contents

Flower Bath Scrub	2
Posey Scrubby	3
Soap Pocket	4
Hexagon Crochet Dishcloth	5
Zen Scrubby Poufs	6
Turtle Bath Scrubby	8
Spa Day Crochet	10
Shiny Scrubby Monster	11
Rubber Duckie	12
Happy Face Scrubby Emoticons	14
Shark Puppet Scrubby	16
Happy Hippo Face Scrubby	18
Friendly Lion Face Scrubby	20
Cute Chickie Scrubby	22
Fancy Flower Scrubber	24
Valentine Scrubby	26
Peppermint Scrubby	27
Jack o' Lantern	28
Snowman Scrubby	30
Santa Scrubby Mitt	32
Retro Ornament Scrubby	34
Happy Sun Scrubby	36
Splash of Citrus Scrubby	38
Cupcake Scrubby	40
Ice Cream Cone Scrubby	42
Strawberry Sparkle Scrubby	44
Cherry Pie Scrubby	46
Sliced Apple Scrubby	48
Fried Egg Scrubby	50
Pear Scrubby	52
Maple Leaf Scrubby	53
Pineapple Scrubby Dishcloth	54
Watermelon Slice Scrubby	56

For pattern inquiries, please visit: www.go-crafty.com

flower bath scrub

Pretty enough to be considered a bathtub décor accessory, this flower-shaped scrubby is wonderful to give as a gift (or crochet for yourself). The textured polyester yarn is great at cleaning without being rough on your skin. It washes easily by machine for cleanliness and reuse-ability.

Yarn
RED HEART® Scrubby™,
3.5 oz (100 g), 92 yd (85 m) balls
- 1 ball of 241 Duckie (A) and 10 Coconut (B)

Hook
Susan Bates® Crochet Hook:
5 mm (US H-8)

Other
- Yarn needle

LEARN BY VIDEO
www.go-crafty.com

Ch (chain)
Dc (double crochet)
Slip stitch
Sc (single crochet)

Designed by Michele Wilcox

GAUGE
3 dc = 1" (2.5 cm). Gauge is not critical for this project.

MEASUREMENTS
Daisy measures 8" (20.5 cm) in diameter.

DAISY
With A, ch 4.

Round 1 (right side): Work 11 dc in 4th ch from hook; join with slip st in top of beginning ch-4—12 dc.

Round 2: Ch 3 (counts as dc here and throughout), dc in first st, 2 dc in each dc around; join with slip st in top of beginning ch-3—24 dc.

Round 3: Ch 3, 2 dc in next dc, *dc in next dc, 2 dc in next dc; repeat from * around; join with slip st in top of beginning ch-3—36 dc.

Round 4: Slip st around the post of beginning ch-3 in preceding round, *ch 7, slip st around post of next dc in same round, turn, work 10 sc over ch-7 loop, turn, skip loop just made, slip st around the post of next dc*; repeat from * to * around; join with slip st in top of beginning ch-3—18 ch-7 loops.

Round 5: Repeat Round 4 in sts of Round 2—12 loops.

Round 6: Repeat Round 4 in sts of Round 1—6 loops.
Fasten off.

Border
With right side facing, working from behind, join B with a slip st to any dc in Round 3.

Round 1: Ch 3, 2 dc in first st, 3 dc in each dc around; join with slip st in top of beginning ch-3—108 dc.

Round 2: *Skip next 2 dc, 5 dc in next dc, skip next 2 dc, sc in next dc; repeat from * around—18 shells.
Fasten off. Weave in ends. ■

posey scrubby

This handy scrubby will brighten your time washing the dishes! Crochet it with just three simple rounds and then add a scallop edging round. It's perfect in the bathroom too!

Yarn
RED HEART® Scrubby Sparkle™ solids, 3 oz (85 g), 174 yd (159 m) balls
- 1 ball 8215 Lemon

Hook
Susan Bates® Crochet Hook: 4.25 mm (US G-6)

Other
- Yarn needle

LEARN BY VIDEO
www.go-crafty.com

Ch (chain)
Sc (single crochet)
Dc (double crochet)
Hdc (half double crochet)
Tr (treble crochet)

Designed by Sharon Mann

GAUGE
Gauge is not critical for this project.

MEASUREMENT
Flower measures 4½" (11.5 cm) across.

FLOWER
Ch 4, sc in first ch to form a ring.
Round 1: Ch 3 (counts as dc here and throughout), work 11 dc in ring—12 dc.
Round 2: Ch 3, dc in same st, 2 dc in each st around, slip st in top of beginning ch-3—24 dc.
Round 3: Ch 2 (counts as hdc here and throughout), hdc in same st, 2 hdc in each st around, slip st in top of beginning ch—48 hdc.
Round 4: Sc in same st, hdc in next st, (dc, tr) in next st, (tr, dc) in next st, hdc in next st, sc in next st, *sc in next st, hdc in next st, (dc, tr) in next st, (tr, dc) in next st, hdc in next st, sc in next st; repeat from * around, slip st in first sc—8 petals. Fasten off.

FINISHING
Weave in ends.

soap pocket

Crochet a neat soap pocket for bathing using yarn that gently exfoliates your skin. Choose a color that will please for a thoughtful Scrubby gift. The unique polyester yarn dries easily between uses and can be easily washed in the washing machine.

Yarn
RED HEART® Scrubby™ solids, 3.5 oz (100 g), 92 yd (85 m), prints 3.0 oz (85 g) 78 yd (71 m) balls
• 1 ball 980 Tropical

Hook
Susan Bates® Crochet Hook: 5.5 mm (US I-9)

Other
Yarn needle
1" (25 mm) button
Bar of soap

LEARN BY VIDEO
www.go-crafty.com

Ch (chain)
Sc (single crochet)
Slip stitch
Dc (double crochet)

Designed by Michele Wilcox

GAUGE
Gauge is not critical for this project.

MEASUREMENTS
Pocket measures 3" wide x 5" long (7.5 x 12.5 cm).

POCKET
Ch 8.
Round 1 (right side): Sc in 2nd ch from hook and in next 5 ch, 3 sc in last ch; working in opposite side of foundation ch, skip first ch, sc in next 5 ch, 2 sc in last ch; join with slip st in first sc—16 sc.
Round 2: Ch 3 (counts as first dc here and throughout), 2 dc in same st as join, *skip next sc, 3 dc in next sc; repeat from * 6 times, skip last sc; join with slip st in top of beginning ch—24 dc.
Rounds 3–7: Slip st in next dc, ch 3, 2 dc in same dc, *skip next 2 dc, 3 dc in next dc; repeat from * around, skip last dc; join with slip st in top of beginning ch—eight 3-dc groups.
Round 8: Ch 1, sc in same st as join, sc in next 13 dc, (sc, ch 10, slip st) in next dc, sc in each remaining dc; join with slip st in first sc—24 sc and 1 ch-10 button loop.

FINISHING
Flatten pocket so button loop is centered at back of piece. Sew button to center of front below top edge. Weave in ends. Insert soap in pocket and fasten button loop over button. ■

hexagon crochet dishcloth

What a nice shape to use for your dishwashing! Choose any two colors of Scrubby yarn and crochet this easy kitchen helper. Since it is polyester, it air dries quickly and will wash by machine.

Yarn
RED HEART® Scrubby™,
3.5 oz (100 g), 92 yd (85 m) balls
- 1 ball each 501 Ocean (A) and 905 Cherry (B)

Hook
Susan Bates® Crochet Hook:
5.5 mm (US I-9)

Other
Stitch markers
Yarn needle

▶ **LEARN BY VIDEO**
www.go-crafty.com
Ch (chain)
Slip stitch
Hdc (half double crochet)

Designed by Lorna Miser

GAUGE
13 hdc = 4" [10 cm]; 12 rows = 4" [10 cm] in half double crochet.
CHECK YOUR GAUGE. Use any size hook to obtain the gauge.

MEASUREMENT
Finished Size: 8½" [21.5 cm] diameter

DISHCLOTH
With A, ch 3, slip st in first ch to form a ring.
Round 1: Ch 2 (counts as hdc here and throughout), 11 hdc in ring, slip st in top of beginning ch-2 to join—12 hdc.
Round 2: Ch 3 (counts as hdc and ch 1 here and throughout), hdc in same st, hdc in next st, *(hdc, ch 1, hdc) in next st, hdc in next st; repeat from * around, slip st in 2nd ch of beginning ch-3—18 hdc and 6 ch-1 spaces. Place markers in each ch-1 space to mark corners.
Round 3: Ch 3, hdc in first ch-1 space, hdc in each st to ch-1 space, *(hdc, ch 1, hdc) in next ch-1 space, hdc in each hdc to next ch-1 space; repeat from * around, slip st in 2nd ch of beginning ch-3—30 hdc and 6 ch-1 spaces.
Round 4: Ch 3, hdc in first ch-1 space, hdc in each st to next ch-1 space, *(hdc, ch 1, hdc) in next ch-1 space, hdc in each hdc to next ch-1 space; repeat from * around, slip st in 2nd ch of beginning ch-3—42 hdc and 6 ch-1 spaces. Cut A.
Round 5: Change to B, ch 3, hdc in first ch-1 space, hdc in each st to next ch-1 space, *(hdc, ch 1, hdc) in next ch-1 space, hdc in each hdc to next ch-1 space; repeat from * around, slip st in 2nd ch of beginning ch-3—54 hdc and 6 ch-1 spaces.
Rounds 6–8: Repeat Round 5, working two more hdc between corner ch-1 spaces.
Cut B.
Rounds 9–12: Change to A, repeat Round 5, working two more hdc between corner ch-1 spaces. Fasten off.

FINISHING
Weave in ends.

zen scrubby poufs

Crochet a simple flat Scrubby in the round. Then the outer round is sewn to center to gather it up into a pouf. The soft colors are used as the last round and can be changed up to coordinate with your bathroom décor.

Yarn
RED HEART® Scrubby™ solids, 3.5 oz (100 g), 92 yd (85 m), prints 3.0 oz (85 g) 78 yds (71 m) balls
- 1 ball each 10 Coconut (A), 510 Glacier (B), 215 Bamboo (C), and 805 Stream (D)

Hook
Susan Bates® Crochet Hook: 5.5 mm (US I-9)

Other
Yarn needle

LEARN BY VIDEO
www.go-crafty.com

Ch (chain)
Dc (double crochet)
Slip stitch
Sc (single crochet)

Designed by Laura Bain

GAUGE
Gauge is not critical for this project.

MEASUREMENT
Scrubby measures 4" (10 cm) in diameter, gathered.

NOTES
1 Scrubby is worked in joined rounds with right side facing at all times.
2 Work in spaces between stitches of the previous round and not into the top of each stitch unless otherwise instructed.

SCRUBBY (MAKE 3—1 EACH WITH A & B, A & C, AND A & D)

With A, ch 5.
Round 1: Work 8 dc in 4th ch from hook (beginning ch count as first dc); join with slip st in top of beginning ch—9 dc.
Round 2: Ch 3 (counts as first dc here and throughout), dc in space between first 2 sts, 2 dc in each remaining space around; join with slip st in top of beginning ch—18 dc.
Round 3: Ch 3, dc in space between first 2 sts, *dc in next space, 2 dc in next space; repeat from * around; join with slip st in top of beginning ch—27 dc.
Round 4: Ch 3, dc in space between first 2 sts, *dc in next 2 spaces, 2 dc in next space; repeat from * around; join with slip st in top of beginning ch—36 dc.
Round 5: Ch 3, dc in space between first 2 sts, *dc in next 3 spaces, 2 dc in next space; repeat from * around; join with slip st in top of beginning ch—45 dc.
Round 6: Ch 3, dc in space between first 2 sts, *dc in next 4 spaces, 2 dc in next space; repeat from * around; join with slip st in top of beginning ch—54 dc.
Round 7: Ch 3, dc in each space around; change to 2nd color; join with slip st in top of beginning ch.
Round 8: Ch 1, sc in each space around; join with slip st in first sc. Fasten off, leaving a long tail for sewing.

FINISHING
Thread tail onto yarn needle. Working along Round 8, insert needle into every 9th st and beginning st; pull tight. Insert needle into Round 1 to secure. Fasten off. Weave in ends. ∎

turtle bath scrubby

Crochet this uniquely textured washcloth that kids will love using in the bathtub. It's also great for scrubbing pots in the kitchen.

Yarn
RED HEART® Scrubby™,
3.5 oz (100 g), 98 yd (85 m) balls
- 1 ball each 0561 Grape (A),
  0709 Bubblegum (B),
  0010 Coconut (C), 0241 Duckie (D)

Hook
Susan Bates® Crochet Hook:
5mm (US H-8)

Other
Yarn needle
stitch marker
1 yd (1 m) black worsted-weight yarn
(to embroider eyes)

 LEARN BY VIDEO
www.go-crafty.com

Ch (chain)
Hdc (half double crochet)
Dc (double crochet)
Slip stitch
Sc (single crochet)

Designed by Michele Wilcox

GAUGE
Gauge is not critical for this project.

MEASUREMENT
Scrubby measures 6¼" (16 cm) diameter across shell.

SPECIAL TECHNIQUE
Join with sc: Place a slip knot on hook, insert hook in indicated stitch, yarn over and draw up a loop, yarn over and draw through both loops on hook.

NOTES
1 Shell pieces are made in joined rounds with right side facing. All other pieces are made in continuous rounds (spirals).
2 To change color, work last stitch of old color to last yarn over. Yarn over with new color and draw through all loops on hook to complete stitch. Proceed with new color. Cut old color.

SCRUBBY
Top of Shell
With A, ch 4.
Round 1 (right side): Work 11 dc in 4th ch from hook (beginning ch counts as first dc); change to B; join with slip st in top of beginning ch—12 dc.
Round 2: Ch 3 (counts as first dc here and throughout), dc in same st as join, 2 dc in each dc around; change to C; join with slip st in top of beginning ch—24 dc.
Round 3: Ch 3, 2 dc in next dc, *dc in next dc, 2 dc in next dc; repeat from * around; change to A; join with slip st in top of beginning ch—36 dc.
Round 4: Ch 3, dc in next dc, 2 dc in next dc, *dc in next 2 dc, 2 dc in next dc; repeat from * around; join with slip st in top of beginning ch—48 dc.
Round 5: Ch 2 (counts as first hdc here and throughout), hdc in dc around. Fasten off.

Bottom of Shell
With D, work Rounds 1–5 same as top of shell, do not change colors.

Opening for Hand
Round 1: With wrong sides of shells held together and working through both thicknesses, join B with sc in any hdc, sc in next 35 sts; working through top of shell only, sc in remaining 12 sts; join with slip st in first sc. Fasten off.
Note: For head, legs, and tail, place marker for beginning of round at end of Round 1 and move marker up as each round is completed.

Head
With D, ch 2.
Round 1: Work 6 sc in 2nd ch from hook, do not join—6 sc.
Round 2: Work 2 sc in each sc around—12 sc.
Rounds 3–7: Sc in each sc around; join with slip st in first sc at end of Round 7. Fasten off, leaving a long tail for sewing.

Leg (make 4)
With D, ch 2.
Round 1: Work 6 sc in 2nd ch from hook, do not join—6 sc.
Round 2: *Sc in next sc, 2 sc in next sc; repeat from * twice—9 sc.
Rounds 3–5: Sc in each sc around; join with slip st in first sc at end of Round 5. Fasten off, leaving a long tail for sewing.

Tail
With D, ch 2.
Round 1: Work 6 sc in 2nd ch from hook, do not join—6 sc.

Rounds 2–4: Sc in each sc around; join with slip st in first sc at end of Round 4. Fasten off, leaving a long tail for sewing.

FINISHING

Use photograph as a guide for placement of all pieces.

Head

Holding shell with opening at bottom, center and sew head to closed edge of shell directly opposite opening for hand. With black yarn, embroider 2 French knots for eyes.

Legs

Sew legs evenly spaced apart on underside of shell.

Tail

Center and sew tail at opening for hand on wrong side of top shell.

Weave in ends.

spa day crochet

You deserve a gently exfoliating cloth to pamper yourself as you bathe. These crochet scrubby cloths in softer shades are perfect for relaxing baths or showers. They are the great idea for gift-giving too!

Yarn
RED HEART® Scrubby™ solids, 3.5 oz (100 g), 92 yd (85 m), prints 3.0 oz (85 g) 78 yds (71 m) balls
- 1 ball 215 Bamboo or 805 Stream

Hook
Susan Bates® Crochet Hook: 5.5 mm (US I-9)

Other
Yarn needle

LEARN BY VIDEO
www.go-crafty.com
Ch (chain)
Dc (double crochet)

Designed by Laura Bain

GAUGE
Gauge is not critical for this project.

MEASUREMENTS
Washcloth measures approximately 8" (20.5 cm) wide x 7" (18 cm) long

NOTE
All dc should be worked in space between dc of previous row.

SCRUBBY
Chain 28.
Row 1: Dc in third chain from hook and in each chain across—25 dc. Skipped 2 stitches do not count as first dc.
Row 2: Chain 3 (does not count as a dc here and throughout), turn, work dc in space between each stitch—25 dc. Repeat Row 2 until piece measures 7" (18 cm) from beginning.
Fasten off.

FINISHING
Weave in ends.

shiny scrubby monster

Make wash time more fun with this crocheted monster cloth! This funny-faced friend will get rid of the day's dirt and grime easily and then can be washed by machine with the other washcloths. It air-dries quickly after using or after washing.

Yarn
RED HEART® Scrubby Sparkle™,
3 oz (85 g), 174 yd (159 m) balls
- 1 ball each 8690 Avocado (A), 8506 Ice Pop (B), 8012 Licorice (C), 8215 Lemon (D), and 8001 Marshmallow (E)

Hook
Susan Bates® Crochet Hook: 5.5 mm (US I-9)

Other
Yarn needle

LEARN BY VIDEO
www.go-crafty.com

Ch (chain)
Dc (double crochet)
Adjustable loop/ring
Hdc (half double crochet)

Designed by Laura Bain

GAUGE
12 sts = 4" (10 cm); 10 rows = 4" (10 cm). Gauge is not critical for this project.

MEASUREMENTS
Washcloth measures 9" wide by 6½" long (23 x 16.5 cm).

SPECIAL TECHNIQUE
Adjustable-ring method: Wrap yarn into a ring, ensuring that the tail falls behind the working yarn. Grip ring and tail firmly between middle finger and thumb. Insert hook through center of ring, yarn over (with working yarn) and draw up a loop. Work stitches of first round in the ring, working over both strands (the tail and the ring). After the first round of stitches is worked, pull gently, but firmly, on tail to tighten ring.

NOTES
1 To change color, work last stitch of old color to last yarn over. Yarn over with new color and draw through all loops on hook to complete stitch. Proceed with new color. Cut old color.
2 Eyes are worked in continuous (spiral) rounds. Do not join until instructed.

WASHCLOTH
With A, ch 30.
Row 1: Dc in 4th ch from hook (beginning ch count as first dc) and in each ch across, turn—28 dc.
Row 2: Ch 3 (counts as first dc here and throughout), dc in each dc across, working last dc in top of beginning ch, turn.
Repeat Row 2 until piece measures 4" (10 cm); change to B in last row.
Repeat Row 2 until piece measures 6½" long (16.5 cm). Fasten off.

Eye (make 2)
With C, make an adjustable ring.
Round 1: Ch 2 (counts as first hdc here and throughout), 7 hdc in ring; change to D—8 hdc. Pull on tail to close ring.
Round 2: Ch 2, hdc in same st as join, 2 hdc in each remaining st around; change to E—16 hdc.
Round 3: Ch 2, 2 hdc in next st, *hdc in next st, 2 hdc in next st; repeat from * around; join with slip st in top of beginning ch—24 hdc. Fasten off, leaving a long tail for sewing.

Mouth
With D, ch 10. Fasten off, leaving a long tail for sewing.

FINISHING
Referring to photograph as a guide, sew eyes and mouth on washcloth. Weave in all ends.

rubber duckie

Bath time is rubber duckie time! Crochet these colorful ducks in any color you wish for some sudsy fun. They are easily kept clean by machine washing, and you'll love that this yarn dries more quickly than thick cotton cloths.

Yarn
RED HEART® Scrubby™ solids,
3.5 oz (100 g), 92 yd (85 m) and
RED HEART® Scrubby™ prints,
3 oz (85 g), 78 yd (71 m) balls
- 1 ball each 620 Lime (A),
  241 Duckie (B), and 258 Orange (C)

RED HEART® Super Saver®,
7 oz (198 g), 364 yd (333 m)
- 1 yd of 312 Black (D)

Hook
Susan Bates® Crochet Hook:
5 mm (US H-8)

Other
Yarn needle

 LEARN BY VIDEO
www.go-crafty.com

Ch (chain)
Sc (single crochet)
Sc3tog (single crochet 3
    stitches together)
Sc2tog (single crochet 2
    stitches together)

Designed by Michele Wilcox

GAUGE
Gauge is not critical for this project.

MEASUREMENT
Scrubby measures 7" (18 cm) long, excluding hanging loop.

SPECIAL STITCHES
sc2tog: [Insert hook in next stitch, yarn over and pull up a loop] twice, yarn over and draw through all 3 loops on hook.
sc3tog: [Insert hook in next stitch, yarn over and pull up a loop] 3 times, yarn over and draw through all 4 loops on hook.

SCRUBBY (MAKE 1 EACH WITH A AND B)
Beginning at top of head, ch 6.
Row 1: Sc in 2nd ch from hook and in each ch across, turn—5 sc.
Row 2: Ch 1, 2 sc in first sc, sc in each sc across to last sc, 2 sc in last sc, turn—7 sc.
Row 3: Repeat Row 2—9 sc.
Row 4: Ch 1, sc in each sc across, turn.
Row 5: Repeat Row 2—11 sc.
Rows 6–10: Repeat Row 4.
Row 11: Ch 1, sc3tog, sc in next 5 sc, sc3tog, turn—7 sc.
Row 12: Ch 12, sc in 2nd ch from hook and in each ch across, sc in first 6 sc, 2 sc in last sc, turn—19 sc.
Row 13: Ch 1, 2 sc in first sc, sc in each remaining sc, turn—20 sc.
Row 14: Ch 1, sc in each sc across to last sc, 2 sc in last sc, turn—21 sc.
Row 15: Repeat Row 13—22 sc.
Row 16: Ch 1, sc2tog, sc in each remaining sc, turn—21 sc.
Row 17: Ch 1, sc in each sc across to last 2 sc, sc2tog, turn—20 sc.
Rows 18 and 19: Repeat Rows 16 and 17—18 sc.
Rows 20 and 21: Repeat Row 16—16 sc.
Row 22: Repeat Row 4.
Rows 23 and 24: Ch 1, sc2tog, sc in each sc across to last 2 sc, sc2tog, turn—12 sc.
Round 25: Ch 1, sc2tog, sc in each sc across to last 2 sc, sc2tog; *working in ends of rows and adding sc as needed to keep piece flat, sc in each row* to Row 12; working in opposite side of foundation ch, 3 sc in first ch, sc in each remaining ch, repeat from * to * to Row 1; working in opposite side of foundation ch, 2 sc in first ch, sc in next ch, (sc, ch 9, slip st) in next sc (hanging loop made), sc in next ch, 2 sc in last ch; repeat from * to * around to first sc; join with slip st in first sc. Fasten off.

Beak (make 2)
With C, ch 2.
Row 1: Work 2 sc in 2nd ch from hook, turn—2 sc.
Row 2: Ch 1, sc in each sc across, turn.
Row 3: Ch 1, 2 sc in first sc, sc in last sc, turn—3 sc.
Row 4: Ch 1, sc in first sc, 2 sc in next sc, sc in last sc, turn—4 sc.
Row 5: Repeat Row 2. Leaving a long tail for sewing, fasten off.

FINISHING
With ending tail, sew beak to head. With D, embroider satin stitches for each eye. Weave in ends. ■

happy face scrubby emoticons

Whether you use these in the bathroom or kitchen, they will add a happy note to the job at hand. Crochet them quickly in the round and then add the facial features. They are a great gift for social media fans or someone who makes you smile!

Yarn
RED HEART® Scrubby™, 3.5 oz (100 g), 92 yd (85 m) balls
• 1 ball 241 Duckie (A)

RED HEART® Super Saver®, Art. E300 available in solid color 7 oz (198 g), 364 yd (333 m); prints, multis and heathers 5 oz (141 g), 236 yd (215 m), flecks 5 oz (141 g), 260 yds (238 m) skeins
• 1 skein each 319 Cherry Red (B) and 312 Black (C)

Hook
Susan Bates® Crochet Hook: 5.5 mm (US I-9)

Other
Yarn needle

LEARN BY VIDEO
www.go-crafty.com

Adjustable loop
Ch (chain)
Dc (double crochet)
Slip stitch

Designed by Salena Baca

GAUGE
Gauge is not critical for this project.

MEASUREMENT
Scrubby measures 7½" (19 cm) in diameter.

SPECIAL STITCH
surface slip st (surface slip stitch): With yarn held on wrong side, insert hook in indicated stitch or space, yarn over, pull loop to right side and through loop on hook.

SPECIAL TECHNIQUE
Adjustable-ring method: Wrap yarn in a ring, ensuring that the tail falls behind the working yarn. Grip ring and tail firmly between middle finger and thumb. Insert hook through center of ring, yarn over (with working yarn) and draw up a loop. Work stitches of first round in ring, working over both strands (the tail and the ring). After the first round of stitches is worked, pull gently, but firmly, on tail to tighten ring.

LOVE YA SCRUBBY
With A, make an adjustable loop.
Round 1 (right side): Ch 3 (counts as first dc here and throughout), 11 dc in ring; join with slip st in top of beginning ch—12 dc. Pull gently on beginning tail to close loop.
Round 2: Ch 3, dc in same st as join, 2 dc in each st around; join with slip st in top of beginning ch—24 dc.
Round 3: Ch 3, 2 dc in next st, *dc in next st, 2 dc in next st; repeat from * around; join with slip st in top of beginning ch—36 dc.
Round 4: Ch 3, dc in next st, 2 dc in next st, *dc in next 2 sts, 2 dc in next st; repeat from * around; join with slip st in top of beginning ch—48 dc.
Round 5: Ch 3, dc in next 2 sts, 2 dc in next st, *dc in next 3 sts, 2 dc in next st; repeat from * around; join with slip st in top of beginning ch—60 dc. Fasten off.

Facial Features
Heart-shaped Eye (make 2)
With B, make an adjustable loop.
Round 1 (right side): Ch 3, (3 dc, 3 hdc, ch 1, 3 hdc, 3 dc, ch 3, slip st) in loop—14 dc and 1 ch. Fasten off, leaving a long tail for sewing. Pull gently on beginning tail to close loop.

Mouth
With C, make an adjustable loop.
Row 1 (right side): Ch 3, 5 dc in loop, turn—6 dc.
Row 2: Ch 3, dc in first dc, 2 dc in each remaining st across, turn—12 dc.
Row 3: Ch 3, dc in first dc, dc in next st, *2 dc in next st, dc in next st; repeat from * across—18 dc. Fasten off, leaving a long tail for sewing. Pull gently on beginning tail to close loop.

Finishing
Refer to photograph as a guide and position all pieces with right sides facing. Place eyes and mouth where desired on first scrubby and sew in place.
Weave in ends.

SMILEY FACE SCRUBBY
Work same as Love Ya Scrubby.

Facial Features
Eye (make 2)
With C, make an adjustable loop.
Round 1 (right side): Ch 2 (counts as first hdc), 9 dc in loop; join with slip st in top of beginning ch—10 hdc. Fasten off, leaving a long tail for sewing. Pull gently on beginning tail to close loop.

Smile
Insert hook in any space between Rounds 3 and 4, with yarn held on wrong side of scrubby, place C-colored slip knot on hook and draw through to right side, work 20 surface slip sts loosely between same rounds. Fasten off, drawing end tail to wrong side.

Finishing
Referring to photograph as a guide, position eyes where desired above smile and sew in place.
Weave in ends.

shark puppet scrubby

Make bath time a fun time with this friendly puppet-style scrubby! Kids will love having this clever shark for creative play, while moms will appreciate how you can keep it fresh and clean by just washing by machine.

Yarn
RED HEART® Scrubby™ solids, 3.5 oz (100 g), 92 yd (85 m) balls, and RED HEART® Scrubby™ prints, 3 oz (85 g), 78 yd (71 m) balls
- 1 ball each 510 Glacier (A), 905 Cherry (B), and 10 Coconut (C)

Hook
Susan Bates® Crochet Hook: 5 mm (US H-8)

Other
Yarn needle
2 yd (2 m) black worsted-weight yarn
Sewing needle
White carpet thread

▶ LEARN BY VIDEO
www.go-crafty.com
Ch (chain)
Sc (single crochet)
Sc2tog (single crochet 2 stitches together)

Designed by Michele Wilcox

GAUGE
Gauge is not critical for this project.

MEASUREMENT
Puppet measures 12" (30.5 cm) from tip of nose to end of tail.

SPECIAL STITCH
sc2tog: [Insert hook in next stitch, yarn over and pull up a loop] twice, yarn over and draw through all 3 loops on hook.

SPECIAL TECHNIQUE
Join with sc: Place a slip knot on hook, insert hook in indicated stitch, yarn over and pull up a loop, yarn over and draw through both loops on hook.

NOTE
You may prefer to sew sections together with carpet thread. If carpet thread is used, do not leave long tails for sewing when fastening off.

PUPPET
Top of Body
Beginning at tip of nose, with A, ch 4.
Row 1 (right side): Sc in 2nd ch from hook and in each ch across, turn—3 sc.
Row 2: Ch 1, sc in first sc, 3 sc in next sc, sc in last sc, turn—5 sc.
Rows 3 and 4: Ch 1, sc in first sc, 2 sc in next sc, sc in each sc across to last 2 sc, 2 sc in next sc, sc in last sc, turn—9 sc.
Row 5: Ch 1, sc in first 4 sc, 3 sc in next sc, sc in last 4 sc, turn—8 sc and one 3-sc group.
Rows 6–8: Ch 1, sc in each sc across to center st of 3-sc group, 3 sc in center st, sc in each remaining sc—14 sc and one 3-sc group.
Rows 9–25: Ch 1, sc in each sc across, turn.
Piece should measure about 6½" (16.5 cm) long.
Row 26: Ch 1, sc in first sc, sc2tog, sc in each sc across to last 3 sc, sc2tog, sc in last sc, turn—15 sc.
Rows 27 and 28: Ch 1, sc in each sc across, turn.
Rows 29–31: Repeat Row 26—13 sc.
Fasten off, leaving a long tail for sewing.

Bottom of Body
Front Section
Work same as Rows 1–19 of Top of Body. Fasten off. Piece should measure about 4½" (11.5 cm) long.

Back Section
With A, ch 18.
Row 1 (right side): Sc in 2nd ch from hook and in each ch across, turn—17 sc.
Rows 2–5: Ch 1, sc in each sc across, turn.
Row 6–11: Repeat Rows 26–31 of Top of Body.
Fasten off.

ASSEMBLY
Place Top of Body on a flat surface. Place Back Section of Bottom of Body on Top of Body, matching last row of each section. Sew side edges together. Lay Front Section of Bottom of Body on Top of Body, placing last row of Front Section against first row of Back Section (Front Section will be shorter than Top of Body). Beginning at Row 19 of Front Section and working toward front of puppet, sew edges of Rows 19–25 of Front Section to Top of Body on each side of puppet, leaving remaining rows unsewn for Mouth. Leave last row of Front Section and first row of Back Section unsewn for hand opening.

Mouth
Top
With B, ch 4.
Rows 1–4: Work same as Rows 1–4 of Top of Body—9 sc.
Row 5: Ch 1, sc in each sc across, turn.
Rows 6 and 7: Work same as Rows 6 and 7 of Top of Body—13 sc.
Rows 8–16: Ch 1, sc in each sc across, turn.
Fasten off, leaving a long tail for sewing.

Bottom
Work same as Rows 1–11 of Top of Mouth.
Fasten off.
Sew Row 16 of Top and Row 11 of Bottom together.

Teeth
Holding Mouth open flat with right side facing and working in ends of rows, join C with slip st in any row, *ch 2, slip st in 2nd ch from hook, slip st in next 4 rows; repeat from * around, easing to fit as needed; join with slip st in first slip st. Pin Mouth to Top of Body and Front Section of Bottom of Body. With carpet thread, sew in place.

Tail (make 2)
With A, ch 10.
Row 1 (right side): Sc in 2nd ch from hook and in each ch across, turn—9 sc.
Rows 2 and 3: Ch 1, 2 sc in first sc, sc in each sc across to last sc, 2 sc in last sc, turn—13 sc.
Row 4: Ch 1, sc in each sc across, turn.
Row 5: Ch 1, 2 sc in first sc, sc in next 4 sc, 2 sc in next sc; leave remaining 7 sc unworked, turn—8 sc.

Upper Fin
Rows 6 and 7: Repeat Row 4—8 sc.
Row 8: Ch 1, sc2tog, sc in each sc across to last 2 sc, sc2tog, turn—6 sc.
Row 9: Repeat Row 4.
Row 10: Repeat Row 8—4 sc.
Row 11: Ch 1, [sc2tog] twice, turn—2 sc.
Row 12: Ch 1, sc2tog—1 sc. Fasten off.

Lower Fin
Row 6: With right side of Row 5 facing, skip first unworked sc, join A with sc in next sc, sc in same sc, sc in next 4 sc, 2 sc in last sc, turn—8 sc.
Rows 7–12: Repeat Rows 7–12 of first half.
With wrong sides together, sew Tails together around outer edges. Holding puppet flat on its side, sew Row 1 edges to back of piece.

Top Fin (make 2)
Beginning at bottom edge, with A, ch 8.
Row 1 (right side): Sc in 2nd ch from hook and in each ch across, turn—7 sc.
Row 2: Ch 1, sc in each sc across, turn.
Row 3: Ch 1, sc2tog, sc in each sc across to last sc, 2 sc in last st, turn.
Row 4: Ch 1, 2 sc in first sc, sc in each sc across to last 2 sc, sc2tog, turn.
Row 5: Repeat Row 3.
Row 6: Ch 1, 2 sc in first sc, [sc in next sc, sc2tog] twice, turn—6 sc.
Row 7: Ch 1, skip first sc, [sc2tog] twice, 2 sc in last sc—4 sc. Fasten off, leaving a long tail for sewing.
Sew Top Fins together, then sew piece to top of puppet.

Bottom Fin
With A, ch 6.
Row 1: Sc in 2nd ch from hook and in each ch across, turn—5 sc.
Rows 2 and 3: Work same as Rows 3 and 4 of Top Fin.
Row 4: Ch 1, [sc2tog] twice, 2 sc in last sc—4 sc. Fasten off, leaving a long tail for sewing.
Sew Bottom Fin to Back Section of Bottom of Body.

FINISHING
With black yarn, embroider satin stitches for eyes.
Weave in ends. ■

happy hippo face scrubby

Kids of all ages will enjoy washing up while using this hippo with a charming personality. Crocheted in Scrubby Sparkle, it can be washed by machine and will air dry quickly.

Yarn
RED HEART® Scrubby Sparkle™, 3 oz (85 g), 174 yd (159 m) balls
- 1 ball each 8506 Ice Pop (A) and 8012 Licorice (B)

Note Only a small quantity of B is needed for this project.

Hook
Susan Bates® Crochet Hook: 4 mm (US G-6)

Other
Yarn needle
stitch marker
Sewing needle
Ecru thread

LEARN BY VIDEO
www.go-crafty.com

Ch (chain)
Sc (single crochet)
Slip stitch
Dc (double crochet)

Designed by Michele Wilcox

GAUGE
8 dc = 1½" (4 cm); 3 rows = 1½" (4 cm) in double crochet. CHECK YOUR GAUGE. Use any size hook to obtain the gauge.

MEASUREMENT
Scrubby measures 5½" (14 cm) in diameter.

SPECIAL STITCH
reverse sc (reverse single crochet): Work single crochet in opposite direction from which you would usually work (left to right if you are right handed and right to left if you are left handed). This stitch is also known as crab stitch. It creates a rope-like twisted single crochet edging.

NOTES
1 Head is made in joined rounds with right side facing at all times.
2 Snout is made in continuous (spiral) rounds; do not join until instructed. Place marker for beginning of round and move marker up as each round is completed.

SCRUBBY
Head
With A, ch 6.
Round 1: Sc in 2nd ch from hook and in next 3 ch, 3 sc in last ch; working on opposite side of foundation ch, skip first ch, sc in next 3 ch, 2 sc in last ch; join with slip st in first sc—12 dc.
Round 2: Ch 3 (counts as first dc here and throughout), dc in same st as join, 2 dc in each remaining st around; join with slip st in top of beginning ch—24 dc.
Round 3: Ch 3, 2 dc in next dc, *dc in next dc, 2 dc in next dc; repeat from * around; join with slip st in top of beginning ch—36 dc.
Round 4: Ch 3, dc in next dc, 2 dc in next dc, *dc in next 2 dc, 2 dc in next dc; repeat from * around; join with slip st in top of beginning ch—48 dc.
Round 5: Ch 3, dc in next 2 dc, 2 dc in next dc, dc in next 3 dc, 2 dc in next dc; repeat from * around; join with slip st in top of beginning ch—60 dc.
Round 6: Ch 1, sc in same st as join, sc in next 3 dc, 2 sc in next dc, *sc in next 4 dc, 2 sc in next dc; repeat from * around; join with slip st in top of beginning ch—72 sc. Fasten off.

Ear (make 2)
With A, ch 6; join with slip st in first ch to form a ring.
Round 1: Ch 1, 10 sc in ring; join with slip st in first sc. Fasten off, leaving a long tail for sewing.

Snout
With A, ch 9.
Round 1: Sc in 2nd ch from hook and next 6 ch, 3 sc in last ch; working on opposite side of foundation ch, skip first ch, sc in next 6 ch, 2 sc in last ch—18 sc. Do not join. Place marker for beginning of round and move marker up as each round is completed.
Round 2: Work 2 sc in next sc, sc in next 6 sc, 2 sc in next 3 sc, sc in next 6 sc, 2 sc in last 2 sc—24 sc.
Round 3: *Sc in next 3 sc, 2 sc in next sc; repeat from * around—30 sc.
Round 4: *Sc in next 4 sc, 2 sc in next sc; repeat from * around—36 sc.
Round 5: *Sc in next 5 sc, 2 sc in next sc; repeat from * around—42 sc.
Round 6: *Sc in next 6 sc, 2 sc in next sc; repeat from * around; join with slip st in first sc—48 sc.
Round 7: Ch 1, reverse sc in each st around; join with slip st in first sc. Fasten off.

Eye (make 2)
With B, ch 2.
Round 1: Work 6 sc in 2nd ch from hook; join with slip st in first sc. Fasten off.

FINISHING
Ears With end tails, sew ears to top of head, leaving 10 sts between ears.

Sew remaining pieces to head with sewing needle and thread.

Eyes Tie beginning and end tails together on wrong side of each eye and trim close to knot. Sew eyes in place.

Snout With B, embroider straight stitches for each nostril and short backstitches for smile. Draw beginning and end tails to wrong side of snout and tie together. Trim ends. Align lower edge of snout to lower edge of head and sew snout in place, working stitches through base of each reverse sc.

Trim "eyelash" strands from nostrils and eyes to emphasize their shape.
Weave in ends.

friendly lion face scrubby

With this friendly lion, kids will enjoy bath time, and he will make them smile while washing the dishes! Crochet it in Scrubby Sparkle, and it can be machine washed easily and will air-dry quickly.

Yarn
RED HEART® Scrubby Sparkle™, 3 oz (85 g), 174 yd (159 m) balls
- 1 ball each 8215 Lemon (A), 8260 Orange (B), and 8012 Licorice (C)

Note Only a small quantity of C is needed for this project.

Hook
Susan Bates® Crochet Hook: 4 mm (US G-6)

Other
Yarn needle
Sewing needle
Ecru thread

▶ LEARN BY VIDEO
www.go-crafty.com

Ch (chain)
Dc (double crochet)
Slip stitch
Sc (single crochet)
Hdc (half double crochet)
Sc2tog (single crochet 2 stitches together)

Designed by Michele Wilcox

GAUGE
8 dc = 1½" (4 cm); Rounds 1–3 = 3¼" (8.5 cm). CHECK YOUR GAUGE. Use any size hook to obtain the gauge.

MEASUREMENT
Scrubby measures 6¼" (16 cm) in diameter.

SPECIAL STITCH
sc2tog: [Insert hook in next stitch, yarn over and pull up a loop] twice, yarn over and draw through all 3 loops on hook.

SPECIAL TECHNIQUE
Join with sc: Place a slip knot on hook, insert hook in indicated stitch, yarn over and pull up a loop, yarn over and draw through both loops on hook.

SCRUBBY
Head
With A, ch 4.

Round 1: Work 11 dc in 4th ch from hook (beginning skipped ch count as first dc); join with slip st in top of beginning ch—12 dc.

Round 2: Ch 3 (counts as first dc here and throughout), dc in same st as join, 2 dc in each remaining st around; join with slip st in top of beginning ch—24 dc.

Round 3: Ch 3, 2 dc in next dc, *dc in next dc, 2 dc in next dc; repeat from * around; join with slip st in top of beginning ch—36 dc.

Round 4: Ch 3, dc in next dc, 2 dc in next dc, *dc in next 2 dc, 2 dc in next dc; repeat from * around; join with slip st in top of beginning ch—48 dc.

Round 5: Ch 3, working in back loops only, dc in same st as join, (ch 1, 2 dc) in each remaining st, ch 1; join with slip st in top of beginning ch—96 dc and 48 ch-1 spaces.

Round 6: Ch 3, dc in each dc and ch-1 space around; join with slip st in top of beginning ch—144 dc. Fasten off.

Mane
Round 1: Join B with sc in any unworked front loop of Round 4, *ch 4, dc in 3rd ch from hook and in next ch, skip next 2 front loops, sc in next front loop; repeat from * around; join with slip st in first sc. Fasten off.

Top of Nose
With B, ch 5.

Row 1: Slip st in 2nd ch from hook, sc in next ch, hdc in next ch, dc in last ch. Fasten off.

Bottom of Nose
With C, ch 5.

Row 1: Sc2tog in 2nd and 3rd ch from hook, sc2tog in last 2 ch, turn—2 sc.

Row 2: Ch 1, sc2tog—1 sc. Fasten off.

Eye (make 2)
With C, ch 2.

Round 1: Work 6 sc in 2nd ch from hook; join with slip st in first sc. Fasten off.

FINISHING
Refer to photograph for placement of facial features. Sew all pieces with sewing needle and thread.

Nose Sew top and bottom pieces to center of head.

Eyes Sew in place on Round 2.

Mouth With C, embroider smiling mouth with back stitches under nose.

Trim "eyelash" strands from facial features to emphasize their shape.

Weave in ends. ∎

cute chickie scrubby

This chickie is ready to help wash faces in the bathroom or do dish duty in the kitchen. Crocheted in Scrubby Sparkle, it can be machine washed and will air-dry quickly. She is the perfect gift for an Easter surprise!

Yarn
RED HEART® Scrubby Sparkle™
3 oz (85 g), 174 yd (159 m) balls
- 1 ball each 8215 Lemon (A), 8260 Orange (B), and 8012 Licorice (C)

Note Only small quantities of B and C are needed for this project.

Hook
Susan Bates® Crochet Hook:
5 mm (US H-8)

Other
Yarn needle
Dritz Fray Check® liquid seam sealant

 LEARN BY VIDEO
www.go-crafty.com
Adjustable loop/ring
Ch (chain)
Sc (single crochet)
Dc (double crochet)
Slip stitch
Hdc (half double crochet)
Sc2tog (single crochet 2 stitches together)
Tr (treble crochet)

Designed by Randy Cavaliere

GAUGE
Rounds 1–4 = 2¾" [7 cm]. Gauge is not critical for this project.

MEASUREMENT
Scrubby measures 5¼" (13.5 cm) across diameter.

SPECIAL STITCHES
sc2tog (single crochet 2 together):
[Draw up a loop in next st] twice, yarn over and draw through all 3 loops on hook.

SPECIAL TECHNIQUES
Adjustable ring: Wrap yarn into a ring, ensuring that the tail falls behind the working yarn. Grip ring and tail firmly between middle finger and thumb. Insert hook through center of ring, yarn over (with working yarn) and draw up a loop. Work stitches of first round in the ring, working over both strands (the tail and the ring). After the first round of stitches is worked, pull gently, but firmly, on tail to tighten ring.

Join with sc: Place a slip knot on hook, insert hook in indicated stitch, yarn over and pull up a loop, yarn over and draw through both loops on hook.

Join with slip st: Place a slip knot on hook, insert hook in indicated stitch, yarn over and draw through stitch and loop on hook.

NOTES
1 Scrubby is worked in rounds. Do not join or turn unless instructed.
2 Both Wings and the Head are added as Round 8 is worked.

SCRUBBY
With A, make an adjustable ring.
Round 1 (right side): Ch 1, 8 sc in ring—8 sc. Pull gently on tail to tighten ring and close center.
Round 2: Ch 1, *2 sc in next sc, sc in next sc; repeat from * around—12 sc.
Round 3: Ch 1, 2 sc in each sc around; join with slip st in first sc—24 sc.
Round 4: Ch 4 (counts as first dc, ch 1), dc in same st as join, *skip next sc, (dc, ch 1, dc) in next sc; repeat from * around, skip last dc; join with slip st in 3rd ch of beginning ch-4—24 dc and 12 ch-1 spaces.
Round 5: Ch 1, (sc, hdc, ch 2, slip st) in same st as join (Right Feather made), skip next ch, (slip st, ch 2, hdc, sc) in next dc (Left Feather made), *(sc, hdc, ch 2, slip st) in next dc, skip next ch, (slip st, ch 2, hdc, sc) in next dc; repeat from * around; join with slip st in first sc—12 Right Feathers and 12 Left Feathers.
Fasten off.
Round 6 (wrong side): With wrong side facing and holding yarn between Feathers, join A with sc (see Special Techniques) in any ch-1 space of Round 3, (ch 3, sc) in each ch-1 space around, join with slip st in first sc; turn—24 sc, 12 ch-3 spaces.
Round 7 (right side): Ch 1, slip st in first ch-3 space, ch 3 (counts as first dc), 4 dc in same space, 5 dc in each ch-3 space around; join with slip st in top of beginning ch—60 dc.
Round 8: See Notes above.

First Wing
Ch 7; turn.
Row 1: Sc in 2nd ch from hook and next 5 ch, slip st in next dc; turn—6 sc.
Row 2: Sc in first 4 sc, slip st in next sc, leave last sc unworked, ch 1; turn—4 sc.
Row 3: Skip slip st, sc in next 4 sc, slip st in next dc; turn—4 sc.
Row 4: Sc in first 2 sc, slip st in next sc, leave last sc unworked, ch 1; turn—2 sc.
Row 5: Skip slip st, sc in next 2 sc, slip st in next dc (first Wing made)—2 sc.
Sc in next 9 dc.

Head
Ch 4 (counts as first tr); working from left to right, skip 3 sc to right of current st, slip st in 4th sc; working from right to left, 10 tr in same dc as last sc made (Head made)—11 tr.
Skip next 4 dc, sc in next 4 dc; slip st in next dc.

Second Wing
Ch 3; turn.
Row 1: Sc in 2nd ch from hook and next ch, slip st in next dc; turn—2 sc.

Row 2: Sc in first sc, 2 sc in next sc, ch 2; turn—3 sc.
Row 3: Sc in 2nd ch from hook and in each sc, slip st in next dc; turn—4 sc.
Row 4: Sc in next 3 sc, 2 sc in last sc, ch 2; turn—5 sc.
Row 5: Sc in 2nd ch from hook and in each sc, sc in next dc (second Wing made)—7 sc.
Sc in each remaining 35 dc around; join with slip st in space between last and first dc—43 sc, 2 Wings, one 11-tr Head. Fasten off.

First Foot
With right side facing, join B with sc (see Special Techniques) in 13th sc from second Wing, ch 3, sc in same sc, (sc, ch 3, sc) in next 2 sc—6 sc, 3 ch-3 loops. Fasten off.

Second Foot
With right side facing, skip next 5 sc, join B with sc (see Special Techniques) in next sc, ch 3, sc in same sc, (sc, ch 3, sc) in next 2 sc—6 sc, 3 ch-3 loops. Fasten off.

Beak
With right side facing, join B with sc (see Special Techniques) around post of 6th tr of Head, sc around post of same tr, ch 1, turn, sc2tog. Fasten off.

Comb
Join B with slip st (see Special Techniques) in 5th tr of Head, (ch 3, slip st in 2nd ch from hook and in last ch, slip st) in same tr as join, (sl st, ch 3, slip st in 2nd ch from hook and in last ch, slip st) in next 2 tr—3 sections. Fasten off.

FINISHING
Carefully slide Beak down tr as far as possible. Draw beginning tail to Wrong Side between 5th and 6th tr; draw end tail to Wrong Side through top of same dc as base of tr. Tie tails together without pulling Beak to Wrong Side.

Eyelashes
Using photo as a guide, cut two 8" (20.5 cm) strands of C. With "Eyelashes" pointing up, wrap 1 strand around 4th tr of Head 3 times. Draw tails to Wrong Side and tie together, taking care not to pull so tightly on ends as to pull Eyelashes to Wrong Side. Repeat around 8th tr of Head. With needle, carefully straighten Eyelashes upward bring out fullness. Trim ends of tails close to Head. Weave in ends. Apply sealant to all knots and ends to prevent unraveling. Apply to Eyelashes also, if desired, to seal in place.

fancy flower scrubber

Combining utility with beauty, these flower-shaped scrubbers are wonderful to give as a gift (or crochet for yourself). The textured polyester yarn is great at cleaning without being rough on your skin. It washes easily by machine for cleanliness and reusability.

Yarn
RED HEART® Scrubby™,
3.5 oz (100 g), 92 yd (85 m) balls
- 1 ball each 12 Black (A), 905 Cherry (B), 709 Bubblegum (C), and 501 Ocean (D)

Hook
Susan Bates® Crochet Hook:
5 mm (US H-8)

Other
Yarn needle

LEARN BY VIDEO
www.go-crafty.com

Ch (chain)
Hdc (half double crochet)
Sc (single crochet)
Sc2tog (single crochet 2 stitches together)
Hdc2tog (half double crochet 2 stitches together)
Sc3tog (single crochet 3 stitches together)

Designed by Lorene Eppolite

GAUGE
Gauge is not critical for this project.

MEASUREMENT
Scrubby measures 10½" (26.5) across widest petals.

SPECIAL STITCHES

hdc2tog: [Yarn over, insert hook in next stitch, yarn over and pull up loop] 2 times, yarn over and draw through all 5 loops on hook.

Beg-Fhdc (beginning foundation half double crochet): Yarn over, insert hook in indicated stitch and pull up a loop, yarn over and draw through one loop on hook (the "chain"); yarn over and draw through 3 loops on hook (the "half double crochet").

Fhdc (foundation half double crochet): *Yarn over, insert hook into the "chain" of the previous stitch and pull up a loop, yarn over and draw through one loop on hook (the "chain"); yarn over and draw through 3 loops on hook (the "half double crochet"). Repeat from * for each Fhdc.

sc2tog: [Insert hook in next stitch, yarn over and pull up a loop] twice, yarn over and draw through all 3 loops on hook.

sc3tog: [Insert hook in next stitch, yarn over and pull up a loop] 3 times, yarn over and draw through all 4 loops on hook.

SPECIAL TECHNIQUE

Join with sc: Place a slip knot on hook, insert hook in indicated stitch, yarn over and draw up a loop, yarn over and draw through both loops on hook.

NOTES

1 Scrubby is worked in continuous (spiral) rounds with right side facing.
2 Scrubby is intended for frequent use and washing. Designer recommends tying tails together at color change to prevent unraveling.
3 To change color, work last stitch of old color to last yarn over. Yarn over with new color and draw through all loops on hook to complete stitch. Proceed with new color. Cut old color. Work over tails to minimize weaving in.

SCRUBBY (MAKE 3—1 EACH WITH A & B, A & C, AND A & D)

With A, ch 3.

Round 1 (right side): Work 9 hdc in 3rd chain from hook (beginning ch counts as first hdc); join with slip st in top of beginning ch—10 hdc.

Round 2: Ch 1, 2 hdc in each hdc around; join with slip st in first hdc—20 hdc.

Round 3: Ch 1, *hdc in next hdc, 2 hdc in next hdc; repeat from * around; join with slip st in first hdc—30 hdc. Fasten off.

Round 4: With right side facing, join 2nd color with sc in any hdc, sc in next 3 hdc, *Beg-Fhdc in next hdc, Fhdc 4 times, ch 3, hdc in base of each of the 5 Fhdc just made, hdc in next hdc, sc in next 4 hdc; repeat from * around to last 2 hdc, Beg-Fhdc in next hdc, Fhdc 4 times, ch 3, hdc in base of each of the 5 Fhdc just made, hdc in last hdc; join with slip st in first sc—20 sc, 25 Fhdc, 25 hdc, and 5 ch-3 spaces.

Round 5: Ch 1, *sc in next sc, sc2tog, sc in next sc, hdc in next 5 Fhdc, 4 hdc in next ch-3 space, hdc in next 5 hdc; repeat from * around; join with slip st in first sc—15 sc and 70 hdc.

Round 6: Ch 1, *sc in next 3 sc, hdc2tog, hdc in next 2 hdc, 2 dc in next 6 hdc, hdc in next 2 hdc, hdc2tog; repeat from * around; join with slip st in first sc—15 sc, 30 hdc, and 60 dc.

Round 7: Ch 1, *sc3tog, dc in next 3 hdc, dc in next 3 dc, 2 dc in next 6 dc, dc in next 3 dc, dc in next 3 hdc; repeat from * around; join with slip st in first sc. Fasten off.

FINISHING
Weave in ends. ■

valentine scrubby

Give this heart-shaped Scrubby as a gift to make dishwashing or bathing a time for the recipient to remember that they are loved. Choose from any of the wonderful shades of this yarn—no one says crochet hearts have to be red!

Yarn
RED HEART® Scrubby™,
3.5 oz (100 g), 92 yd (85 m) balls
• 1 ball each 905 Cherry (A) and 709 Bubblegum (B)

Hook
Susan Bates® Crochet Hook:
4mm (US G-6)

Other
Yarn needle

LEARN BY VIDEO
www.go-crafty.com

Ch (chain)
Dc (double crochet)
Dc2tog (double crochet 2 stitches together)
Sc (single crochet)

Designed by Michele Wilcox

GAUGE
Gauge is not critical for this project.

MEASUREMENTS
Scrubby measures 9" wide x 8½" long (23 x 21.5 cm).

SPECIAL STITCH
dc2tog: [Yarn over, insert hook in next stitch, yarn over and pull up loop, yarn over, draw through 2 loops] 2 times, yarn over, draw through all 3 loops on hook.

SPECIAL TECHNIQUE
Join with sc: Place a slip knot on hook, insert hook in indicated stitch, yarn over and pull up a loop, yarn over and draw through both loops on hook.

SCRUBBY
With A, ch 4.
Row 1 (right side): Work 5 dc in 4th ch from hook (beginning ch counts as first dc), turn—6 dc.
Rows 2–10: Ch 3 (counts as first dc here and throughout), dc in first dc (same as base of beginning ch-3), dc in each st across to beginning ch, 2 dc in top of beginning ch, turn—24 dc.
Row 11: Ch 3, dc in each dc across, turn.

First Lobe
Row 12: Ch 3, dc in next 11 dc; leave remaining sts unworked, turn—12 dc.
Rows 13–15: Ch 3, dc2tog, dc in each st to last 3 sts, dc2tog, dc in top of beginning ch, turn—6 dc.
Fasten off.

2nd Lobe
Row 12 (wrong side): With wrong side facing, skip first unworked st, join A with slip st in next unworked st, ch 3, dc in each remaining st across, turn—12 dc.
Rows 13–15: Repeat Rounds 13–15 of first lobe. Do not fasten off at end of last round.

Edging
Round 1: Ch 1, working in ends of rows, sts, and opposite side of foundation ch, sc evenly spaced around, adding sc as needed to keep piece flat and working 3 sc in foundation ch (base of 6 dc of Row 1); join with slip st in first sc. Fasten off.
Round 2: With right side facing, join B with sc in center st of 3-sc group at bottom of piece, *ch 2, skip next sc, sc in next sc; repeat from * around, adding sc as need to keep piece flat; join with slip st in first sc. Do not turn.
Round 3: Ch 1, (sc, ch 3, sc) in each ch-2 space around; join with slip st in first sc. Fasten off.

FINISHING
Weave in ends.

peppermint scrubby

Freshen up your kitchen or scrub those plates clean with this festive crocheted helper. It's even great for washing your face! This unique polyester yarn can be washed by machine and air-dries quickly. Make them for the perfect hostess gift or stocking stuffer.

Yarn
RED HEART® Scrubby™,
3.5 oz (100 g), 92 yd (85 m) balls
- 1 ball each 905 Cherry A and 10 Coconut B.

Hook
Susan Bates® Crochet Hook:
4 mm (US G-6)

Other
Yarn needle

▶ LEARN BY VIDEO
www.go-crafty.com
Ch (chain)
Slip stitch
Dc (double crochet)
Sc (single crochet)

Designed by Sharon Mann

GAUGE
Gauge is not critical for this project.

MEASUREMENT
Scrubby measures about 8" [20.5 cm] diameter, not including hanging loop.

NOTES
1. Scrubby is worked in joined rounds, with same side facing at all times. Do not turn at the end of rounds.
2. To change color, work last stitch of old color to last yarn over. Yarn over with new color and draw through all loops on hook to complete the stitch. Proceed with new color. Cut old color.

PINWHEEL
With A, ch 4; join with slip st in first ch to form a ring.

Round 1: With A, ch 3 (counts as first dc here and throughout), work 11 more dc in ring, changing to B in last dc; join with slip st in 3rd ch of beginning ch-3—12 dc.

Round 2: With B, ch 3, dc in same st as joining, 2 dc in each of remaining 11 sts, changing to A in last dc; join with slip st in 3rd ch of beginning ch-3—24 dc.

Round 3: With A, ch 3, 2 dc in next st, [dc in next st, 2 dc in next st] 11 times, changing to B in last dc; join with slip st in 3rd ch of beginning ch-3—36 dc.

Round 4: With B, ch 3, dc in same st as joining, 2 dc in next st, dc in next st, [2 dc in next 2 sts, dc in next st] 11 times, changing to A in last dc; join with slip st in 3rd ch of beginning ch-3—60 dc.

Round 5: With A, ch 3, 2 dc in next st, [dc in next st, 2 dc in next st] 29 times, changing to B in last dc; join with slip st in 3rd ch of beginning ch-3—90 dc.

Round 6: With B, ch 3, dc in each st around, changing to A in last st; join with slip st in 3rd ch of beginning ch-3.

Round 7: With A, ch 1, sc in same st as joining, skip next st, [2 sc in next st, skip next st] 44 times; join with slip st in first sc.

Hanging Loop
With A, ch 12, slip st in same st as joining; leave remaining sts unworked.
Fasten off.

FINISHING
Weave in ends. ■

jack o' lantern

This happy pumpkin has a sparkling personality thanks to the Scrubby Sparkle yarn! He's fun to crochet and give as an alternative to sweet treats for Halloween. He's perfect for use in the bath or at the kitchen sink!

Yarn
RED HEART® Scrubby Sparkle™,
3 oz (85 g), 174 yd (159 m) balls
- 1 ball each of 8260 Orange (A), 8690 Avocado (B), 8012 Licorice (C)

Hook
Susan Bates Crochet Hook®:
4.0 mm (US G-6)

Other
Yarn needle

 LEARN BY VIDEO
www.go-crafty.com

Ch (chain)
Sc (single crochet)
Sc2tog (single crochet 2 stitches together)

Designed by Michele Wilcox

GAUGE
16 sc and 10 rows sc = 4" (10 cm). CHECK YOUR GAUGE. Use any size hook to obtain the gauge.

MEASUREMENTS
Scrubby measures: 7¾" x 7¾" (19.7 x 19.7 cm)

SPECIAL STITCH
sc2tog: [Draw up a loop in next st] twice, yarn over and draw through all 3 loops on hook.

PUMPKIN
With A, beginning at bottom Edge, ch 13.
Row 1 (wrong side): Sc in second ch from hook and each ch across; turn—12 sc.
Row 2 (right side): Ch 1 (does not count as a stitch), sc in first sc, 2 sc in next sc, sc in each sc across to last 2 sc, 2 sc in next sc, sc in last sc; turn—14 sc.
Row 3: Ch 1, sc in first sc, 2 sc in next sc, sc in each of next 3 sc, 2 sc in each of next 4 sc, sc in each of next 3 sc, 2 sc in next sc, sc in last sc; turn—20 sc.
Rows 4–9: Repeat Row 2—32 sc.
Rows 10–19: Ch 1, sc in each sc across; turn.
Row 20: Ch 1, sc in first sc, sc2tog, sc in each sc across to last 3 sc, sc2tog; sc in last sc; turn—30 sc.
Rows 21–25: Repeat Row 20—20 sc.

Right Top
Row 26: Ch 1, sc in first sc, sc2tog, sc in each of next 4 sc, sc2tog, sc in next sc; turn, leaving last 10 sts unworked—8 sc.
Row 27: Ch 1, sc2tog, sc in each of next 4 sc, sc2tog; turn—6 sc.
Row 28: Ch 1, sc2tog, sc in each of next 2 sc, sc2tog; turn—4 sc. Fasten off.

Left Top
Referring to photo for placement, join A in first unworked sc at center of Row 25.
Row 29: Ch 1, sc in first sc, sc2tog, sc in each of next 4 sc, sc2tog, sc in last sc; turn—8 sc.
Row 30: Ch 1, sc2tog, sc in each of next 4 sc, sc2tog; turn—6 sc.
Row 31: Ch 1, sc2tog, sc in each of next 2 sc, sc2tog; turn—4 sc. (Do not fasten off.)

EDGE
With right side facing, ch 1, sc around outside edge of pumpkin, working sts into sides of Rows as needed to keep work flat, and working a slip st in the bottom of the top center "V." Fasten off yarn and weave in ends.

STEM
With B, ch 5.
Row 1: Sc in second ch from hook and each ch across; turn—4 sc.
Rows 2–3: Ch 1, sc in each sc across; turn—4 sc.
Row 4: Ch 1, 2 sc in first sc, sc in each of next 2 sc, 2 sc in last sc; turn—6 sc.
Rows 5–6: Ch 1, sc in each sc across; turn—6 sc.
Row 7: Ch 1, sc in first sc, 2 sc in next sc, sc in each of next 2 sc, 2 sc in next sc, sc in last sc—8 sc. Fasten off, leaving a long end for sewing.
Referring to photo for placement, sew stem to pumpkin.

EYE (MAKE 2)
With C, ch 5.
Row 1: Sc in second ch from hook and each ch across; turn—4 sc.
Row 2: Ch 1, sc in each sc across; turn—4 sc.
Row 3: Ch 1, sc2tog twice; turn—2 sts.
Row 4: Ch 1, sc2tog—1 st.
Fasten off, leaving a long end for sewing. Referring to photo for placement, sew eyes in place with Row 4 at the top of each.

NOSE
Make nose same as eye. Referring to photo for placement, sew nose in place with Row 1 at the top.

MOUTH
With C, ch 6.
Row 1: Sc in second ch from hook and each ch across; turn—5 sc.
Row 2: Ch 1, 2 sc in first sc, sc in each of next 3 sc, 2 sc in last sc; turn—7 sc.
Row 3: Ch 1, 2 sc in first sc, sc in each of next 5 sc, 2 sc in last sc; turn—9 sc. Fasten off, leaving a long end for sewing.
Referring to photo for placement, sew Mouth in place.

FINISHING
Weave in ends.

snowman scrubby

Whether you use him in the bath or at the kitchen sink, this jolly fellow can't help but make it more fun! He's crocheted with this unique polyester yarn that can be washed by machine and air-dries quickly. He's the perfect hostess gift or stocking stuffer.

Yarn
RED HEART® Scrubby™,
3.5 oz (100 g), 92 yd (85 m) balls
- 1 ball each 10 Coconut (A), 620 Lime (B), and 905 Cherry (C), and small amounts of 258 Orange (D), and 12 Black (E)

Hook
Susan Bates® Crochet Hook:
5.5 mm (US I-9)

Other
Yarn needle

LEARN BY VIDEO
www.go-crafty.com

Ch (chain)
Dc (double crochet)
Slip stitch
Fpdc (front post double crochet)
Bpdc (back post double crochet)
Dc2tog (double crochet 2 stitches together)
Sc (single crochet)
Sc2tog (single crochet 2 stitches together)

Designed by Michele Wilcox

GAUGE
Gauge is not critical for this project.

MEASUREMENT
Scrubby measures about 6" (15 cm) across face and 8½" (21.5 cm) long, not including hanging loop.

NOTES
Scrubby is worked in nine pieces that are sewn together to form snowman. The mouth is embroidered with French knots.

SPECIAL STITCHES
Bpdc (back post double crochet): Yarn over, insert hook from back side of work to front and to back again around the post of indicated stitch; yarn over and pull up a loop (3 loops on hook), yarn over and draw through 2 loops (2 loops on hook), yarn over and draw through 2 loops (1 loop on hook). Skip the stitch "in front of" the Bpdc.

Fpdc (Front post double crochet): Yarn over, insert hook from front side of work to back and to front again around post of indicated stitch, yarn over and pull up a loop (3 loops on hook), yarn over and draw through 2 loops (2 loops on hook), yarn over and draw through 2 loops (1 loop remains on hook). Skip the stitch "behind" the Fpdc.

Fpsc (front post single crochet): Insert hook from front to back and to front again around post of indicated stitch, yarn over and draw up a loop, yarn over and draw through 2 loops on your hook. Skip the stitch "behind" the Fpsc.

dc2tog (double crochet 2 stitches together): [Yarn over, insert hook in next stitch, yarn over and pull up loop, yarn over, draw through 2 loops] 2 times, yarn over, draw through all 3 loops on hook.

sc2tog: [Insert hook in next stitch, yarn over and pull up a loop] twice, yarn over and draw through all 3 loops on hook.

HEAD
With A, ch 4.

Round 1: Work 11 dc in 4th ch from hook (3 skipped ch count as first dc); join with slip st in top of beginning ch-3—12 dc.

Round 2: Ch 3 (counts as first dc here and throughout), Fpdc around beginning ch of Round 1, 2 Fpdc around each of next 11 sts; join with slip st in top of beginning ch-3—24 dc.

Round 3: Ch 3, 2 Fpdc around next st, [Fpdc around next st, 2 Fpdc around next st] 11 times; join with slip st in top of beginning ch-3—36 dc.

Round 4: Ch 3, Fpdc around next st, 2 Fpdc around next st, [Fpdc around each of next 2 sts, 2 Fpdc around next st] 11 times; join with slip st in top of beginning ch-3—48 dc.

Round 5: Ch 3, Fpdc around each of next 2 sts, 2 Fpdc around next st, [Fpdc around each of next 3 sts, 2 Fpdc around next st] 11 times; join with slip st in top of beginning ch-3—60 dc.

Round 6: Ch 3, Fpdc around each of next 3 sts, 2 Fpdc around next st, [Fpdc around each of next 4 sts, 2 Fpdc around next st] 11 times; join with slip st in top of beginning ch-3—72 dc.

Round 7: Ch 1, Fpsc around beginning ch-3 of Round 6, Fpsc around each remaining st; join with slip st in first st. Fasten off.

EYE (MAKE 2)
With E, ch 4, slip st in first ch. Cut yarn, leaving a long tail. Pull the long tail all the way through the slip st and pull tightly. Using photograph as a guide, sew eyes to head taking care to work sewing stitches near the surface so they do not show on back of head.

HAT (MAKE 2)
Cuff (make 1 for each hat)
With C, ch 18.
Row 1: Dc in 4th ch from hook (3 skipped ch count as first dc) and in each ch across—16 dc.
Rows 2 and 3: Ch 3 (counts as first dc), turn, [Fpdc around next st, Bpdc around next st] 7 times, dc in top of beginning ch-3.
Fasten off, leaving a long tail for sewing.

Top (make 1 for each hat)
With B, ch 18.
Row 1: Dc in 4th ch from hook (3 skipped ch count as first dc) and in each ch across—16 dc.
Rows 2 and 3: Ch 3 (counts as first dc here and throughout), turn, dc in each st across.
Row 4: Ch 3, turn, [dc2tog] 7 times, dc in top of beginning ch-3—9 dc.
Row 5: Ch 3, turn, [dc2tog] 3 times, dc in next st, dc in top of beginning ch-3—6 dc.
Fasten off, leaving a long tail for sewing.

Assembly
Sew a cuff to long straight edge of each hat top, overlapping the edges slightly. Using matching yarn colors, sew side edges of cuff/top pieces together, leaving lower edges unsewn. Place hat on head and sew in place.

HANGING LOOP
With C, ch 7; join with slip st in first ch to form a ring. Work 14 sc in ring. Fasten off, leaving a long tail for sewing. Sew hanging loop to top center of hat.

FINISHING
Weave in ends.

MOUTH
With E, using photograph as a guide, embroider 7 French knots in a curve for smile.
Cover (to hide French knots on back of head): With A, ch 13. Dc in 4th ch from hook and in each ch across. Fasten off, leaving a long tail for sewing. Sew cover to back of head, covering the back of the French knots.

NOSE
With D, ch 7.
Row 1: Sc in 2nd ch from hook and in each ch across—6 sc.
Row 2: Ch 1, turn, sc in first sc, sc2tog, sc in last 3 sc—5 sc.
Row 3: Ch 1, turn, sc in first sc, sc2tog, sc in last 2 sc—4 sc.
Row 4: Ch 1, turn, [sc2tog] twice—2 sc.
Fasten off, leaving a long tail for sewing. Sew side edges together to form a cone. Using photograph as a guide, sew nose to head.

santa scrubby mitt

Crochet this Scrubby for a jolly host/hostess gift or stocking stuffer! It's great for protecting your holiday manicure whether you use it in the kitchen or bath.

Yarn
RED HEART® Scrubby™ solids, 3.5 oz (100 g), 92 yd (85 m), and RED HEART® Scrubby™ prints, 3 oz (85 g), 78 yd (71 m) balls
- 1 ball each 10 Coconut (A), 215 Bamboo (B), 905 Cherry (C), and 715 Primrose (D)

Hook
Susan Bates® Crochet Hook: 5 mm (US H-8)

Other
Tapestry needle
Sewing needle
White thread
½ yd (½ m) black worsted weight yarn

LEARN BY VIDEO
www.go-crafty.com

Ch (chain)
Sc (single crochet)
Sc2tog (single crochet 2 stitches together)
Hdc (half double crochet)

Designed by Michele Wilcox

GAUGE
Gauge is not critical for this project.

MEASUREMENTS
Mitt measures 5½" (14 cm) across face x 8½" (21.5 cm) long, excluding hanging loop.

SPECIAL STITCH
sc2tog: [Insert hook in next stitch, yarn over and pull up a loop] twice, yarn over and draw through all 3 loops on hook.

NOTES
1 Scrubby is made from front and back pieces worked in turned rows and sewn together.
2 To change color, work last stitch of old color to last yarn over. Yarn over with new color and draw through all loops on hook to complete stitch. Proceed with new color. Cut old color.

MITT
Front
Ribbed Cuff
With A, ch 8.
Row 1 (right side): Sc in 2nd ch from hook and in each ch across, turn—7 sc.
Rows 2–16: Ch 1, working in back loops only, sc in each sc across, turn.

Beard
Row 1 (right side): Ch 1, working in ends of rows, sc in each row across, turn—16 sc.
Row 2: Ch 1, sc in first 7 sc, 2 sc in next sc, sc in next 7 sc, 2 sc in next sc, turn—18 sc.
Row 3: Ch 1, sc in each sc across, turn.
Repeat Row 3 until piece measures 3½" (9 cm) from bottom edge of ribbed cuff; change to B at end of last row.

Face
Repeat Row 3 until piece measures 4¾" (12 cm) from bottom edge of ribbed cuff; change to A at end of last row.
Repeat Row 3 three times; leaving a long beginning tail for sewing, change to C at end of last row.

Hat
Rows 1 and 2: Repeat Row 3 of beard.
Row 3: Ch 1, sc2tog, sc in each sc across to last 2 sc, sc2tog, turn—16 sc.
Row 4: Repeat Row 3 of beard.
Rows 5–12: Repeat last 2 rows 4 times—8 sc at end of Row 12.
Rows 13 and 14: Ch 1, [sc2tog] across, turn—2 sc at end of Row 14.
Fasten off.

Back
Work same as front, omitting all color changes except C for hat.

Mustache
With A, ch 10.
Row 1 (right side): Slip st in 2nd ch from hook, hdc in next ch, 3 dc in next ch, hdc in next ch, slip st in next ch, hdc in next ch, 3 dc in next ch, hdc in next ch, slip st in last ch.
Fasten off.

Nose
With D, ch 2.
Round 1: Work 6 sc in 2nd ch from hook; join with slip st in first sc. Fasten off.

Hanging Loop
With A, ch 10; join with slip st in first ch to form a ring.
Round 1: Ch 1, 12 sc in ring; join with slip st in first sc. Fasten off, leaving a long tail for sewing.

FINISHING
Refer to photograph as a guide for placement of facial features. With sewing needle and thread, sew mustache to center of face above beard and sew nose to head above mustache. With black yarn, embroider satin stitch eye on each side of nose on face.
Taking care to match colors and leaving bottom edge open for wearer's hand, sew front and back together with A-colored across side edges of cuff, beard, and face and with C-colored tails across side edges of hat.
With end tail, sew hanging loop to top point of hat.
Weave in ends.

retro ornament scrubby

This scrubby was inspired by a vintage glass ornament shape. It's crocheted with unique polyester yarn that can be washed by machine and air-dries quickly. It's an ideal hostess gift or stocking stuffer!

Yarn
RED HEART® Scrubby™, 3.5 oz (100 g), 92 yd (85 m) balls
- 1 ball each 258 Orange (A), 709 Bubblegum (B), and 905 Cherry (C)

Hook
Susan Bates® Crochet Hook:
4 mm (US G-6)

Other
Yarn needle

LEARN BY VIDEO
www.go-crafty.com

Ch (chain)
Slip stitch
Dc (double crochet)
Hdc (half double crochet)
Bpdc (back post double crochet)

Designed by Sharon Mann

GAUGE
Gauge is not critical for this project.

MEASUREMENTS
Scrubby measures about 5" (12.5 cm) wide and widest and 6" (15 cm) tall, not including hanging loop.

SPECIAL STITCHES
Cl (2 treble crochet cluster): *[Yarn over] twice, insert hook in indicated stitch, yarn over and draw up a loop, [yarn over and draw through 2 loops on hook] twice; repeat from * once more, yarn over and draw through all 3 loops on hook.
Bpdc (back post double crochet): Yarn over, insert hook from back side of work to front and to back again around the post of indicated stitch; yarn over and pull up a loop (3 loops on hook), [yarn over and draw through 2 loops on hook] twice. Skip the stitch "in front of" the Bpdc.

SPECIAL TECHNIQUE
Join with Bpdc (join with back post double crochet): Place slip knot on hook, yarn over, insert hook from back side of work to front and to back again around the post of indicated stitch; yarn over and pull up a loop (3 loops on hook), [yarn over and draw through 2 loops on hook] twice. Skip the stitch "in front of" the Bpdc.

COLOR SEQUENCE FOR ORNAMENT #1
Work 1 round each with A, B, A, C, C, and B.

COLOR SEQUENCE FOR ORNAMENT #2
Work 1 round each with C, A, C, B, A, and C.

NOTES
1. Scrubby is worked in joined rounds, with same side facing at all times. Do not turn at the end of rounds
2. Yarn quantities are sufficient to make both ornaments.
3. To change color, work last stitch of old color to last yarn over. Yarn over with new color and draw through all loops on hook to complete the stitch. Proceed with new color. Cut old color.

ORNAMENT (MAKE 2—1 IN EACH COLOR SEQUENCE)
With first color, ch 4; join with slip st in first ch to form a ring.
Round 1 (right side): Ch 3 (counts as first dc), work 11 more dc in ring, changing to 2nd color in last dc; join with slip st in 3rd ch of beginning ch-3—12 dc.
Round 2: Ch 3 (counts as first hdc, ch 1), hdc in next st, [ch 1, hdc in next st] 10 times, ch 1 and change to 3rd color; join with slip st in 2nd ch of beginning ch-3—12 hdc and 12 ch-1 spaces.
Round 3: Ch 2 (counts as first hdc), 2 hdc in next ch-1 space, [hdc in next st, 2 hdc in next ch-1 space] 11 times, changing to 4th color in last hdc; join with slip st in 2nd ch of beginning ch-2—36 hdc.
Round 4: Ch 3, dc in same st as joining, dc in next 2 sts, [2 dc in next st, dc in next 2 sts] 11 times, do not change color; join with slip st in 3rd ch of beginning ch-3—48 dc.
Fasten off.
Round 5: With right side facing, join 5th color with Bpdc around any st, Bpdc around each remaining st and change to 6th color in last st; join with slip st in top of first Bpdc—48 Bpdc.
Round 6: Ch 2 (counts as hdc), hdc in same st as joining, hdc in next st, [2 hdc in next st, hdc in next st] 10 times, dc in next st, tr in next st, Cl in each of next 2 sts, tr in next st, dc in next st, [2 hdc in next st, hdc in next st] 10 times; join with slip st in 2nd ch of beginning ch—69 sts.
Do not fasten off.

Hanging Loop
Ch 12, slip st in same st as joining.
Fasten off.

FINISHING
Weave in ends. ■

happy sun scrubby

Make dish washing duties a bit brighter with this cheerful crocheted Scrubby. The sunny face will also encourage children to wash thoroughly in the bathroom.

Yarn
RED HEART® Scrubby™ solids, 3.5 oz (100 g), 92 yd (85 m), and RED HEART® Scrubby™ prints, 3 oz (85 g), 78 yd (71 m) balls
- 1 ball each 241 Duckie (A) and 258 Orange (B)

RED HEART® Super Saver®, 7 oz (198 g), 364 yd (333 m) skeins
- 2 yds (2 m) of 312 Black C

Hook
Susan Bates® Crochet Hook: 5.5 mm (US I-9)

Other
Yarn needle

LEARN BY VIDEO
www.go-crafty.com

Ch (chain)
Dc (double crochet)
Slip stitch
Hdc (half double crochet)
Sc (single crochet)

Designed by Laura Bain

GAUGE
Gauge is not critical for this project.

MEASUREMENT
Scrubby measures 9" (23 cm) across widest points.

SPECIAL TECHNIQUE
Join with sc: Place a slip knot on hook, insert hook in indicated stitch, yarn over and pull up a loop, yarn over and draw through both loops on hook.

NOTES
1 Center of scrubby is worked in joined rounds with right side facing at all times; rays are worked in turned rows.
2 Work all half double crochet and double crochet stitches in spaces between stitches in previous rounds.
3 To change color, work last stitch of old color to last yarn over. Yarn over with new color and draw through all loops on hook to complete stitch. Proceed with new color. Cut old color.

SCRUBBY
With A, ch 4.
Round 1: Work 8 dc in 4th ch from hook (beginning ch count as first dc); join with slip st in top of beginning ch—9 dc.
Round 2: Ch 3 (counts as first dc here and throughout), dc in space between first 2 sts, 2 dc in each remaining space around; join with slip st in top of beginning ch—18 dc.
Round 3: Ch 3, dc in space between first 2 sts, dc in next space, *2 dc in next space, dc in next space; repeat from * around; join with slip st in top of beginning ch—27 dc.
Round 4: Ch 3, dc in space between first 2 sts, dc in next 2 spaces, *2 dc in next space, dc in next 2 spaces; repeat from * around; join with slip st in top of beginning ch—36 dc.
Round 5: Ch 3, dc in space between first 2 sts, *dc in next 2 spaces, 2 dc in next space; repeat from * to last 2 spaces, dc in next space, 2 dc in last space; join with slip st in top of beginning ch; change to B—49 dc.
Round 6: Ch 2 (counts as first hdc), hdc in each space around; join with slip st in top of beginning ch. Fasten off.

Sun Rays
Ray 1
Row 1 (right side): With right side facing, join B with sc in any st, sc in next 6 sts; leave remaining sts unworked, turn—7 sc.
Row 2: Ch 1, sc in each st across to last st; leave last st unworked, turn—6 sc.
Rows 3–6: Repeat Row 2—2 sc at end of Row 6.
Row 7: Ch 1, sc in each st, ch 4, turn, slip st in first sc made (hanging loop made)—2 sc and hanging loop. Fasten off.

Rays 2–7
Row 1 (right side): With right side facing, join B with sc in next unworked st, sc in next 6 sts; leave remaining sts unworked, turn—7 sc.
Rows 2–7: Repeat Row 2 of Ray 1—1 sc at end of Row 7.
Fasten off.

FINISHING
With right side facing, hanging loop at top, and C, embroider satin stitches for eyes and back stitches for smiling mouth. Weave in ends.

splash of citrus scrubby

You'll love these citrus rounds for washing dishes or scrubbing the sink! This textured yarn has a sparkle effect, is easy to crochet with, and can be thrown in the washing machine to keep it fresh.

Yarn
RED HEART® Scrubby Sparkle™, 3 oz (85 g) 174 yd (159 m) balls
- 1 ball each 8260 Orange (A), 8215 Lemon (B), 8690 Avocado (C), and 8001 Marshmallow (D)

Hook
Susan Bates® Crochet Hook: 4 mm (US G-6)

LEARN BY VIDEO
www.go-crafty.com

Ch (chain)
Dc (double crochet)
Fpdc (front post double crochet)
Sc (single crochet)

Designed by Michele Wilcox

GAUGE
Rounds 1–4 = 3¾" (9.5 cm) in double crochet. Exact gauge is not critical for this project.

MEASUREMENT
Scrubby measures 7½" (19 cm) in diameter.

SPECIAL STITCH
Fpdc (Front post double crochet): Yarn over, insert hook from front side of work to back and to front again around post of indicated stitch; yarn over and pull up a loop (3 loops on hook), yarn over and draw through 2 loops (2 loops on hook), yarn over and draw through 2 loops (1 loop on hook).

SPECIAL TECHNIQUE
Join with sc: Place a slip knot on hook, insert hook in indicated stitch, yarn over and pull up a loop, yarn over and draw through both loops on hook.

NOTE
To change color, work last stitch of old color to last yarn over. Yarn over with new color and draw through all loops on hook to complete stitch. Proceed with new color. Cut old color.

SCRUBBY (MAKE 1 EACH WITH A, B, AND C)
Ch 4.
Round 1: Work 11 dc in 4th ch from hook; join with slip st in top of beginning ch—12 dc.
Round 2: Ch 3 (counts as first dc here and throughout), Fpdc around first dc, *dc in next dc, Fpdc around same dc; repeat from * around; join with slip st in top of beginning ch—24 dc.
Round 3: Ch 3, dc in next dc, Fpdc around same dc, *dc in next 2 dc, Fpdc around last dc worked; repeat from * around; join with slip st in top of beginning ch—36 dc.
Round 4: Ch 3, dc in next 2 dc, Fpdc around last dc worked, *dc in next 3 dc, Fpdc around last dc worked; repeat from * around; join with slip st in top of beginning ch—48 dc.
Round 5: Ch 3, dc in next 3 dc, Fpdc around last dc worked, *dc in next 4 dc, Fpdc around last dc worked; repeat from * around; join with slip st in top of beginning ch—60 dc.
Round 6: Ch 3, dc in next 4 dc, Fpdc around last dc worked, *dc in next 5 dc, Fpdc around last dc worked; repeat from * around; join with slip st in top of beginning ch—72 dc.
Round 7: Ch 3, dc in next 5 dc, Fpdc around last dc worked, *dc in next 6 dc, Fpdc around last dc worked; repeat from * around; change to D; join with slip st in top of beginning ch—84 dc.
Round 8: Ch 1, sc in first 6 dc, 2 sc in next dc, *sc in next 6 dc, 2 sc in next dc; repeat from * around; join with slip st in first sc—96 sc.
Fasten off.
Round 9: Working in back loops only, join first color with sc in back loop of first sc, sc in each sc around, (slip st, ch 10, slip st) in first sc (hanging loop made), turn, slip st in each ch; join with slip st in same sc. Fasten off.

FINISHING
Weave in ends.

cupcake scrubby

Add sweetness to your dishwashing time with a delicious looking cupcake scrubby. Crochet it as a treat to yourself or give it with some nice hand lotion. Sweet!

Yarn
RED HEART® Scrubby™ solids, 3.5 oz (100 g), 92 yd (85 m), or RED HEART® Scrubby™ prints, 3 oz (85 g) 78 yds (71 m) balls
- 1 ball each 709 Bubblegum (A), 10 Coconut (B), 905 Cherry (C), 938 Almond (D) and 241 Duckie (E)

Hook
Susan Bates® Crochet Hook: 6 mm (US J-10)

Other
Yarn needle

LEARN BY VIDEO
www.go-crafty.com

Ch (chain)
Dc (double crochet)
Hdc (half double crochet)
Fpdc (front post double crochet)
Bpdc (back post double crochet)
Sc (single crochet)
Hdc2tog (half double crochet 2 stitches together)

Designed by Marly Bird

GAUGE
Gauge is not critical for this project.

MEASUREMENT
Scrubby measures 5" (13 cm) across at widest point.

SPECIAL ABBREVIATIONS
Bpdc (back post double crochet): Yo, insert hook from back to front then to back, going around post of indicated st, draw up a loop, [yo and draw through 2 loops on hook] twice. Skip st in front of the Bpdc.
Fpdc (front post double crochet): Yo, insert hook from front to back then to front, going around post of indicated st, draw up a loop, [yo and draw through 2 loops on hook] twice. Skip st behind the Fpdc.
hdc2tog: [Yarn over, insert hook in next stitch, yarn over and pull up loop] 2 times, yarn over and draw through all loops on hook.
Shell: 5 dc in same stitch.

NOTE
Each part of Scrubby is made separately and then pieces are sewn together.

CUPCAKE
With A, ch 18.
Set-Up Row (wrong side): Dc in 4th ch from hook and in each ch across—15 dc.
Row 1: Ch 2 (does not count as stitch here and throughout), turn, hdc in first st, Fpdc, *Bpdc, Fpdc; repeat from * to last st, hdc in last st.
Row 2: Ch 2, turn, hdc in first st, Bpdc, *Fpdc, Bpdc; repeat from * to last st, hdc in last st.
Repeat Rows 1–2 twice more, then Row 1 once. Fasten off.

FROSTING
Edge
With B, ch 18.
Row 1 (right side): Sc in 2nd ch from hook, [skip next ch, Shell in next ch, skip next ch, sc in next ch] 5 times, turn to work along opposite side of foundation ch, ch 1, *sc in next sc, sc in skipped ch, sc in Shell, sc in skipped ch; repeat from * to last st, sc in last st. Fasten off.
Repeat to make a second edge, do not fasten off.
Joining Row (right side): Holding wrong sides of Edges together with sts of last row matching up, using yarn from second Edge piece and working through both layers to join, ch 1, sc 17 sts evenly spaced across last row.
Rows 2–3: Ch 2, turn, 2 hdc in first st, hdc in each st to end—19 hdc.
Rows 4–5: Ch 2, turn, hdc in each st to end.
Row 6: Ch 2, turn, hdc2tog, hdc in each st to last 2 sts, hdc2tog—17 hdc.
Rows 7–8: Hdc2tog, *hdc, hdc2tog; repeat from * to end—7 hdc.
Row 9: Hdc2tog, hdc in next st, [hdc2tog] twice. Fasten off.

CHERRY
With C, ch 4, slip st in first ch to form a ring.
Round 1: Ch 1, work 10 sc in ring. Fasten off.

STEM
With D, ch 10. Fasten off.

FINISHING
Fit last row of Cupcake in between lower scalloped edges of joined Frosting pieces and sew pieces together.

Sew Cherry in center of top edge of Frosting.

Fold Stem in half and sew ends to top edge of Frosting.

With A and E, embroider straight stitch sprinkles randomly around Frosting. Weave in ends.

ice cream cone scrubby

Cleaning up after an ice cream party is easy with the help of this cleverly designed crochet scrubby! You'll love how quickly it dries between uses and that it can be machine washed to keep it fresh and clean.

Yarn
RED HEART® Scrubby™ solids, 3.5 oz (100 g), 92 yd (85 m), or RED HEART® Scrubby™ prints, 3 oz (85 g) 78 yds (71 m) balls
- 1 ball each 938 Almond (A), 934 Candy (B), 510 Glacier (D), 10 Coconut (C), and 905 Cherry (D)

Hook
Susan Bates® Crochet Hook: 6 mm (US J-10)

Other
Yarn needle

LEARN BY VIDEO
www.go-crafty.com

Ch (chain)
Dc (double crochet)
Sc (single crochet)
Hdc (half double crochet)
Hdc2tog (half double crochet 2 stitches together)

Designed by Marly Bird

GAUGE
Gauge is not critical for this project.

MEASUREMENT
Scrubby measures 5" (13 cm) across at widest point.

SPECIAL ABBREVIATIONS
hdc2tog: [Yarn over, insert hook in next stitch, yarn over and pull up loop] 2 times, yarn over and draw through all loops on hook.
Shell: 5 dc in same stitch.

NOTE
Each part of Scrubby is made separately and then pieces are sewn together.

CONE (MAKE 2)
With A, ch 4.
Set-Up Row (wrong side): Dc in 4th ch from hook.
Row 1: Ch 3 (does not count as a dc here and throughout), turn, 3 dc in dc—3 dc.
Row 2: Ch 3, turn, dc in next 2 dc, 2 dc in last st—4 dc.
Row 3: Ch 3, turn, dc in each dc to last dc, 2 dc to last dc—5 dc.
Repeat Row 3 four more times—9 dc.
Fasten off.

ICE CREAM
First Scoop
With B, ch 14.
Row 1 (right side): Sc in 2nd ch from hook, [skip next ch, Shell in next ch, skip next ch, sc in next ch] 3 times, turn to work along opposite side of foundation ch, ch 1, *sc in sc, sc in skipped ch, sc in Shell, sc in skipped ch; repeat from * to last st, sc in last st.
Rows 2–3: Working along straight edge only, ch 2 (does not count as a hdc here and throughout), turn, 2 hdc in first st, hdc in each st to end—15 hdc.
Fasten off.

Second Scoop
With C, ch 16.
Row 1 (right side): Sc in 2nd ch from hook, sc in next ch, [skip next ch, Shell in next ch, skip next ch, sc in next ch] 3 times, sc in last ch, turn to work along opposite side of foundation ch, ch 1, sc in sc, *sc in next sc, sc in skipped ch, sc in Shell, sc in skipped ch; repeat from * to last 2 sts, sc in last 2 sts.
Rows 2–3: Working along straight edge only, ch 2, turn, hdc2tog, hdc in each st to end—13 hdc.
Fasten off.

Third Scoop
With D, ch 16.
Row 1 (right side): Sc in 2nd ch from hook, sc in next ch, [skip next ch, Shell in next ch, skip next ch, sc in next ch] 3 times, sc in last ch, turn to work along opposite side of foundation ch, ch 1, sc in sc, *sc in next sc, sc in skipped ch, sc in Shell, sc in skipped ch; repeat from * to last 2 sts, sc in last 2 sts.
Rows 2–6: Working along straight edge only, ch 2, turn, hdc2tog, hdc in each st to last 2 sts, hdc2tog—3 hdc.
Fasten off.

CHERRY
With D, ch 4, slip st in first ch to form a ring.
Round 1: Ch 1, work 10 sc in ring.
Fasten off.

STEM
With A, ch 10. Fasten off.

FINISHING
Sew Cone pieces together. Following photo and overlapping pieces along lower scalloped edges, sew three Scoops together.

Sew Ice Cream along top edge of Cone.

Sew Cherry in center of top edge of Third Scoop.

Fold Stem in half and sew ends to top edge of Third Scoop.

Weave in ends.

strawberry sparkle scrubby

Since this scrubby is a double thickness, it's a nice sturdy scrubber for any cleaning task (and you can embroider the seeds while hiding the thread between the layers). Crochet it to help you in the kitchen, then throw it in the washer and air dry.

Yarn
RED HEART® Scrubby Sparkle™, 3 oz (85 g), 174 yd (159 m) balls
- 1 ball each 8929 Strawberry (A) and 8690 Avocado (B)

Hook
Susan Bates® Crochet Hook: 5.5 mm (US I-9)

Other
Yarn needle
8 stitch markers (optional)
½ yd (½ m) black worsted weight yarn

▶ LEARN BY VIDEO
www.go-crafty.com

Ch (chain)
Sc (single crochet)
Sc2tog (single crochet 2 stitches together)
Hdc (half double crochet)
Hdc2tog (half double crochet 2 stitches together)
Sc3tog (single crochet 3 stitches together)

Designed by Nancy Anderson

GAUGE
Gauge is not critical for this project.

MEASUREMENTS
Strawberry measures 5½" wide x 6½" long (14 x 16.5 cm).

SPECIAL STITCH

hdc2tog: [Yarn over, insert hook in next stitch, yarn over and pull up loop] 2 times, yarn over and draw through all 5 loops on hook.

sc2tog: [Insert hook in next stitch, yarn over and pull up a loop] twice, yarn over and draw through all 3 loops on hook.

NOTES

1 Strawberry is made with 2 layers for durability. Leaf cap is a single layer folded and joined to top of strawberry.
2 You may prefer to place a stitch marker on beginning chains of each odd-numbered row of leaf cap so chains are more visible in Row 17.

SCRUBBY
Strawberry
Side 1

With A, ch 9.

Row 1 (right side): Sc in 2nd ch from hook and in each ch across, turn—8 sc.
Row 2: Ch 1, sc in first st, 2 sc in next st, sc in 4 sts, 2 sc in next st, sc in last st, turn—10 sc.
Row 3: Ch 1, sc in first 4 sts, 2 sc in next st, sc in next 4 sts, 2 sc in last st, turn—12 sc.
Row 4: Ch 1, sc in first 5 sts, 2 sc in next st, sc in next 5 sts, 2 sc in last st, turn—14 sc.
Row 5: Ch 1, sc in each st across, turn.
Row 6: Ch 1, sc in first 6 sts, 2 sc in next st, sc in next 6 sts, 2 sc in last st, turn—16 sc.
Row 7: Repeat Row 5.
Row 8: Ch 1, sc in first st, 2 sc in next st, sc in next 3 sts, 2 sc in next st, sc in next st, [2 sc in next st] twice, sc in next st, 2 sc in next st, sc in next 3 sts, 2 sc in next st, sc in last st, turn—22 sc.
Row 9: Repeat Row 5.
Row 10: Ch 1, sc in first st, sc2tog, sc in next 16 sts, sc2tog, sc in last st, turn—20 sc.
Row 11: Repeat Row 5.
Row 12: Ch 1, sc in first 2 sts, [sc2tog, sc in next 5 sts] twice, sc2tog, sc in last 2, turn—17 sc.
Row 13: Repeat Row 5.
Row 14: Ch 1, sc in first st, sc2tog, sc in next 11 sts, sc2tog, sc in last st, turn—15 sc.
Row 15: Ch 1, sc in first 2 sts, sc2tog, sc in next 7 sts, sc2tog, sc in last 2 sts, turn—13 sc.
Row 16: Repeat Row 5.
Row 17: Ch 1, sc in first 2 sts, sc2tog, sc in next 5 sts, sc2tog, sc in last 2 sts, turn—11 sc.
Row 18: Repeat Row 5.
Row 19: Ch 1, skip first st, sc in next 7 sts, sc2tog, sc in last st, turn—9 sc.
Row 20: Ch 1, skip first st, sc in next 6 sts, sc2tog, turn—7 sc.
Row 21: Ch 1, sc in first 2 sts, sc2tog, sc in last 3 sts, turn—6 sc.
Row 22: Ch 1, [sc2tog] 3 times. Fasten off.

Side 2

Work same as Side 1; do not fasten off at end of last row.

Edging

Round 1: With wrong sides of Sides held together and working through both thicknesses, ch 1, turn, 3 sc in each st of Row 22; working in ends of rows, work 21 sc evenly spaced down first side; working in opposite side of foundation ch, sc in first 2 ch, skip next ch, 3 sc in next ch, skip next ch, sc in next 2 ch, skip last ch; working in ends of rows, work 19 sc evenly spaced up 2nd side; join with slip st in first sc. Fasten off.

Leaf Cap

With B, ch 4.

Row 1: Hdc in 2nd ch from hook and in each ch across, turn—3 hdc.
Row 2: Ch 2 (counts as first hdc here and throughout), skip first st, hdc2tog—1 leaf.
Row 3: Ch 4, hdc in 2nd ch from hook and in each ch across, turn.
Row 4: Repeat Row 2.
Rows 5–16: Repeat last 2 rows 6 times—8 leaves at end of Row 16.
Row 17: Ch 1, working in opposite side of foundation ch of each odd-numbered row, sc in each ch across, turning every other leaf so foundation ch are facing, turn—24 sc.
Row 18: Ch 1, sc in each st across, turn.
Row 19: Ch 1, sc in first 2 sts, sc2tog, [sc in next 2 sts, sc2tog] 5 times, turn—18 sc.
Row 20: Ch 1, sc in each st across. Fasten off, leaving a long tail for sewing.

FINISHING

With points of leaves facing downward and top edges even, fold leaf cap in half and wrap around strawberry. Working through all 3 thicknesses, sc in each st across top row—9 sc. Fasten off, but do not cut; use remaining length of tail to tack points of leaves in place.

For seeds, with black yarn, embroider ¼" (6.35 mm) straight stitches randomly through both layers, drawing the yarn between the layers as needed to position seeds wherever desired.
Weave in ends.

cherry pie scrubby

Next time you are invited to dinner or a dessert party, bring along a cherry pie scrubby for your host. The unique crocheted texture is perfect for quickly cleaning dishes, pots, and even the kitchen sink. The polyester fiber dries easily and can be washed by machine to keep it fresh.

Yarn
RED HEART® Scrubby™ solids, 3.5 oz (100 g), 92 yd (85 m), or RED HEART® Scrubby™ prints, 3 oz (85 g) 78 yds (71 m) balls
- 1 ball each 938 Almond (A), 709 Bubblegum (B), 10 Coconut (C), and 905 Cherry (D)

Hook
Susan Bates® Crochet Hook: 6 mm (US J-10)

Other
Yarn needle

▶ LEARN BY VIDEO
www.go-crafty.com

Ch (chain)
Dc (double crochet)
Hdc (half double crochet)
Fpdc (front post double crochet)
Bpdc (back post double crochet)
Sc (single crochet)
Hdc2tog (half double crochet 2 stitches together)

Designed by Marly Bird

GAUGE
Gauge is not critical for this project.

MEASUREMENT
Scrubby measures 7½" [19 cm] across at widest point.

NOTE
Each part of Scrubby is made separately and then pieces are sewn together.

SPECIAL ABBREVIATIONS
Bpdc (back post double crochet): Yo, insert hook from back to front then to back, going around post of indicated st, draw up a loop, [yo and draw through 2 loops on hook] twice. Skip st in front of the Bpdc.
Fpdc (front post double crochet): Yo, insert hook from front to back then to front, going around post of indicated st, draw up a loop, [yo and draw through 2 loops on hook] twice. Skip st behind the Fpdc.
hdc2tog: [Yarn over, insert hook in next stitch, yarn over and pull up loop] 2 times, yarn over and draw through all loops on hook.
Shell: 5 dc in same stitch.

CRUST
With A, ch 18.
Set-Up Row (wrong side): Dc in 4th ch from hook and in each ch across—15 dc.
Row 1: Ch 2 (does not count as stitch here and throughout), turn, hdc in first st, Fpdc, *Bpdc, Fpdc; repeat from * to last st, hdc in last st.
Row 2: Ch 2, turn, hdc in first st, Bpdc, *Fpdc, Bpdc; repeat from * to last st, hdc in last st.
Repeat Rows 1–2 once more, then Row 1 once. Fasten off.

PIE
With B, ch 22.
Row 1 (right side): Sc in 2nd ch from hook, [skip next ch, Shell in next ch, skip next ch, sc in next ch] 5 times, turn to work along opposite side of foundation ch, ch 1, *sc in next sc, sc in skipped ch, sc in Shell, sc in skipped ch; repeat from * to last st, sc in last st.
Rows 2–3: Working along straight edge only, ch 2, turn, hdc in each st to end—21 hdc.
Row 4: Ch 2, turn, [hdc2tog] twice, hdc in each st to last 4 sts, [hdc2tog] twice—17 hdc.
Row 5: Ch 2, turn, hdc2tog, *hdc in next st, hdc2tog; repeat from * to end—11 hdc.
Row 6: Ch 2, turn, [hdc2tog] twice, hdc in next 2 sts, [hdc2tog] twice, hdc in last st—7 hdc.
Row 7: Ch 2, turn, [hdc2tog] twice, hdc in next st, hdc2tog—4 hdc. Fasten off.

CREAM TOP
With C, ch 14.
Row 1 (right side): Sc in 2nd ch from hook, [skip next ch, Shell in next ch, skip next ch, sc in next ch] 3 times, turn to work along opposite side of foundation ch, ch 1, *sc in sc, sc in skipped ch, sc in Shell, sc in skipped ch; repeat from * to last st, sc in sc.
Row 2: Working along straight edge only, ch 2, turn, [hdc2tog] 3 times, hdc in next st, [hdc2tog] 3 times—7 hdc.
Row 3: Ch 2, turn, [hdc2tog] twice, hdc in next st, hdc2tog—4 hdc. Fasten off.

CHERRY
With D, ch 4, slip st in first ch to form a ring.
Round 1: Ch 1, work 10 sc in ring. Fasten off.

STEM
With A, ch 10. Fasten off.

FINISHING
Sew lower scalloped edge of Pie along last row of Crust. With scalloped edge as lower edge, sew Cream centered along top edge of Pie. Sew Cherry in center of top edge of Cream. Fold Stem in half and sew ends to top edge of Cream.

Weave in ends.

sliced apple scrubby

You will love how this little helper makes quick work of sticky kitchen cleanups! Crocheted in fast-drying polyester Scrubby, it washes easily by machine and dries quickly.

Yarn
RED HEART® Scrubby™ solids, 3.5 oz (100 g), 92 yd (85 m), or RED HEART® Scrubby™ prints, 3 oz (85 g), 78 yd (71 m) balls
- 1 ball each of 10 Coconut (A), 905 Cherry (B), 620 Lime (C), and 12 Black (D)

Note: Only a small quantity of D is needed for this project.

Hook
Susan Bates® Crochet Hook: 5 mm (US H-8)

Other
Yarn needle
Stitch marker
Fabric sealant (optional)

LEARN BY VIDEO
www.go-crafty.com

Ch (chain)
Hdc (half double crochet)
Sc (single crochet)
Sc2tog (single crochet 2 stitches together)

Designed by Nancy Anderson

GAUGE
Gauge is not critical for this project.

MEASUREMENTS
Scrubby measures 6" wide x 6½" long (15 x 16.5 cm), excluding leaf and stem.

SPECIAL STITCH
sc2tog: [Insert hook in next stitch, yarn over and pull up a loop] twice, yarn over and draw through all 3 loops on hook.

SPECIAL TECHNIQUE
Join with sc: Place a slip knot on hook, insert hook in indicated stitch, yarn over and pull up a loop, yarn over and draw through both loops on hook.

SCRUBBY
Apple
With A, ch 7.

Round 1: Work 3 hdc in 2nd ch from hook, hdc in next 4 ch, 3 hdc in last ch; working in opposite side of foundation ch, skip first ch, hdc in next 4 ch; join with slip st in first hdc—14 hdc.

Round 2: Ch 2 (counts as first hdc here and throughout), hdc in same st as join, 2 hdc in next 2 sts, hdc in next 4 sts, 2 hdc in next 3 sts, hdc in next 4 sts; join with slip st in top of beginning ch—20 hdc.

Round 3: Ch 2, hdc in same st as join, 2 hdc in next st, hdc in next 2 sts, 2 hdc in next 3 sts, hdc in next 3 sts, 2 hdc in next 2 sts, hdc in next 2 sts, 2 hdc in next 2 sts, hdc in next 3 sts, 2 hdc in last st; join with slip st in top of beginning ch—30 sts.

Round 4: Ch 2, hdc in same st as join, hdc in next 2 sts, *2 hdc in next st, hdc in next 4 sts; repeat from * around; join with slip st in top of beginning ch—36 hdc.

Round 5: Ch 2, hdc in same st as join, hdc in next 5 sts, *2 hdc in next st, hdc in next 5 sts; repeat from * around; join with slip st in top of beginning ch—42 hdc.

Round 6: Ch 2, hdc in same st as join, hdc in next 6 sts, *2 hdc in next st, hdc in next 6 sts; repeat from * around; join with slip st in top of beginning ch—48 hdc. Fasten off.

Round 7: Join B with sc in any st, sc in same st, sc in next 7 sts, *2 sc in next st, sc in next 7 sts; repeat from * around; join with slip st in first sc—56 sc. Fasten off.

Leaf
With C, ch 2.

Row 1 (right side): Work 3 sc in 2nd ch from hook, turn—3 sc.

Row 2: Ch 1, sc in first st, 2 sc in next st, sc in last st, turn—4 sc.

Row 3: Ch 1, *sc in first st, 2 sc in next st; repeat from * once, turn—6 sc.

Row 4: Ch 1, sc in first 2 sts, 2 sc in next 2 sts, sc in last 2 sts, turn—8 sc.

Rows 5 and 6: Ch 1, sc in each st across.

Row 7: Ch 1, skip first st, sc in next st, [sc2tog] 3 times—4 sc. Fasten off, leaving a long tail for sewing.

Stem
With D, ch 6.

Row 1: Sc in 2nd ch from hook and in each ch across—5 sc. Fasten off, leaving a long tail for sewing.

FINISHING
Referring to photograph as a guide, sew stem and leaf to top of apple. With D, embroider seeds ½" (1.5 cm) in length in center of apple, working 2 straight stitches in same place for each seed. Pull beginning and end tails to wrong side of piece and knot. Optional: Apply a drop or 2 of fabric sealant on each knot to prevent unraveling.

Weave in ends.

fried egg scrubby

Dishes with stuck-on eggs easily come clean with the help of this aptly shaped crochet Scrubby! It's the perfect helper for washing stuck on messes in the kitchen. Keep it fresh by washing by machine and it will quickly air dry.

Yarn
RED HEART® Scrubby™ solids, 3.5 oz (100 g), 92 yd (85 m), or RED HEART® Scrubby™ prints 3 oz (85 g), 78 yd (71 m) balls
- 1 ball each 241 Duckie (A) and 10 Coconut (B)

Hook
Susan Bates® Crochet Hook: 5 mm (US H-8)

Other
Yarn needle
Stitch marker

LEARN BY VIDEO
www.go-crafty.com

Ch (chain)
Sc (single crochet)
Slip stitch
Hdc (half double crochet)

Designed by Nancy Anderson

GAUGE
Gauge is not critical for this project.

MEASUREMENTS
Scrubby measures 6" wide x 6½" long (15 x 16.5 cm).

NOTES
1 Scrubby is worked in joined rounds unless otherwise stated.
2 Last 3 rounds are unjoined. Place marker on first stitch and move up as each round is completed.
3 To change color, work last stitch of old color to last yarn over. Yarn over with new color and draw through all loops on hook to complete stitch. Proceed with new color. Cut old color.

SCRUBBY
With A, ch 2.

Round 1: Work 6 sc in 2nd ch from hook; join with slip st in first st—6 sc.
Round 2: Ch 1, 2 sc in each st around; join with slip st in first st—12 sc.
Round 3: Ch 1, sc in first st, 2 sc in next st, *sc in next st, 2 sc in next st; repeat from * around; join with slip st in first st—18 sc.
Round 4: Ch 1, sc in first 2 sts, 2 sc in next st, *sc in next 2 sts, 2 sc in next st; repeat from * around; change to B; join with slip st in first st—24 sts.
Round 5: Ch 1, working in back loops only, sc in first 3 sts, 2 sc in next st, *sc in next 3 sts, 2 sc in next st; repeat from * around; join with slip st in first st—30 sc.
Round 6: Ch 1, sc in first 4 sts, 2 sc in next st, [sc in next 4 sts, 2 sc in next st] twice, [hdc in next 4 sts, 2 hdc in next st] 3 times; join with slip st in first st—36 sc.
Round 7: Ch 1, sc in first 5 sts, 2 sc in next st, [sc in next 5 sts, 2 sc in next st] twice, [hdc in next 5 sts, 2 hdc in next st] 3 times, hdc in space between last and first st; join with slip st in first st—43 sts.
Round 8: Ch 1, sc in first 6 sts, 2 sc in next st, [sc in next 6 sts, 2 sc in next st] twice, [hdc in next 6 sts, 2 hdc in next st] 3 times, 2 hdc in last st, do not join—50 sts. Place marker on first st and move up as rounds are completed.
Round 9: [Sc in next 3 sts, 2 sc in next st, sc in next 4 sts] 3 times, [hdc in 3 sts, 2 hdc in next st, hdc in next 4 sts] 3 times, 2 hdc in next st, 2 sc in last st, do not join—58 sts.
Round 10: Sc in next st, 2 hdc in next 3 sts, hdc in next st, sc in next 3 sts, slip st in next 3 sts, [sc in next 2 sts, 2 sc in next st] twice, slip st in next 3 sts, sc in next st, hdc in next st, 2 hdc in next 3 sts, hdc in next 3 sts, sc in next 4 sts, slip st in next 5 sts, 2 sc in next st, hdc in next 3 sts, sc in next 4 sts, slip st in next 7 sts, hdc in next 2 sts, slip st in last 4 sts; join with slip st in first sc—67 sts. Fasten off.

FINISHING
Weave in ends.

pear scrubby

Crochet a pear-shaped Scrubby to make quick work of cleaning up dirty pans and dishes. You'll love how easily you can freshen the Scrubby by machine washing and how fast it air-dries.

Yarn
RED HEART® Scrubby™ solids, 3.5 oz (100 g), 92 yd (85 m), or RED HEART® Scrubby™ prints, 3 oz (85 g), 78 yd (71 m) balls
- 1 ball each 241 Duckie (A), 620 Lime (B), and 12 Black (C)

Note: Only small quantities of B and C are needed for this project.

Hook
Susan Bates® Crochet Hook: 5.5 mm (US I-9)

Other
Yarn needle
Stitch marker (optional)

LEARN BY VIDEO
www.go-crafty.com
Ch (chain)
Sc (single crochet)
Sc2tog (single crochet 2 stitches together)

Designed by Rebecca J. Venton

GAUGE
Gauge is not critical for this project.

MEASUREMENTS
Scrubby measures 5" wide x 6½" long (12.5 x 16.5 cm), excluding stem.

NOTE
Bottom of pear is worked in continuous rounds. Place marker for beginning of round and move marker up as each round is completed.

SPECIAL STITCH
sc2tog: [Insert hook in next stitch, yarn over and pull up a loop] twice, yarn over and draw through all 3 loops on hook.

SCRUBBY PEAR
Bottom

With A, ch 2.

Round 1: Work 6 sc in 2nd ch from hook—6 sc. Do not join. Place marker for beginning of round and move marker up as each round is completed.

Round 2: Work 2 sc in each st around—12 sc.

Round 3: *Sc in next st, 2 sc in next st; repeat from * around—18 sc.

Round 4: *Sc in next 2 sts, 2 sc in next st; repeat from * around—24 sc.

Round 5: *Sc in next 3 sts, 2 sc in next st; repeat from * around—30 sc.

Round 6: *Sc in next 4 sts, 2 sc in next st; repeat from * around—36 sc.

Round 7: *Sc in next 5 sts, 2 sc in next st; repeat from * around—42 sc.

Round 8: *Sc in next 6 sts, 2 sc in next st; repeat from * around—48 sc. Do not fasten off; remove marker. Continue working in turned rows.

Top

Row 1 (right side): Sc in next 7 sts; leave remaining sts unworked, turn—7 sc.

Row 2: Ch 1, sc in each st across, sc in first unworked st; leave remaining sts unworked, turn—8 sc.

Row 3: Ch 1, sc2tog, sc in next 4 sts, sc2tog, turn—6 sc.

Row 4: Ch 1, sc2tog, sc in next 2 sts, sc2tog, turn—4 sc.

Row 5: Ch 1, [sc2tog] 2 times—2 sc.
Fasten off.

LEAF
With B, ch 7.

Row 1: Sc in 2nd ch from hook, hdc in next ch, dc in next 2 ch, hdc in next ch, sc in last ch, turn—6 sts.

Row 2: Ch 1, sc in first st, hdc in next st, dc in next 2 sts, hdc in next st, sc in next st. Fasten off, leaving a long tail for sewing.

STEM
With C, ch 9.

Row 1: Sc in 2nd ch from hook and in each ch across–8 sc. Fasten off, leaving a long tail for sewing.

FINISHING
Referring to photograph as a guide, sew stem and leaf to top of pear.
Weave in all ends..

maple leaf scrubby

Celebrate Canada or autumn with a crocheted maple leaf Scrubby that shows national pride. Give it to the host of a party or use it in your own kitchen! It's great for cleaning up sticky messes!

Yarn
RED HEART® Scrubby™ solids, 3.5 oz (100 g), 92 yd (85 m), or RED HEART® Scrubby™ prints, 3 oz (85 g), 78 yd (71 m) balls
- 1 ball 905 Cherry

Hook
Susan Bates® Crochet Hook: 5.5 mm (US I-9)

Other
Yarn needle

LEARN BY VIDEO
www.go-crafty.com

Adjustable ring/loop
Ch (chain)
Dc (double crochet)
Slip stitch
Crochet picot
Tr (treble crochet)
Sc (single crochet)

Designed by Salena Baca

GAUGE
Gauge is not critical for this project.

MEASUREMENTS
Scrubby measures 5½" wide x 6" long (14 x 15 cm).

SPECIAL STITCH
Picot: Ch 3, slip st in 3rd ch from hook.

SPECIAL TECHNIQUE
Adjustable-ring method: Wrap yarn in a ring, ensuring that the tail falls behind the working yarn. Grip ring and tail firmly between middle finger and thumb. Insert hook through center of ring, yarn over (with working yarn) and draw up a loop. Work stitches of first round in the ring, working over both strands (the tail and the ring). After the first round of stitches is worked, pull gently, but firmly, on tail to tighten ring.

SCRUBBY
Make an adjustable ring.
Round 1: Ch 2 (counts as first dc here and throughout), 11 dc in ring; join with slip st in top of beginning ch—12 dc.
Round 2: Ch 2, dc in same st as join, 2 dc in each remaining st around; join with slip st in top of beginning ch—24 dc.
Round 3: Ch 2, picot, dc in same st as join, *dc in next st, (dc, picot, dc) in next st, dc in next st, (dc, picot, ch 2, slip st) in next st, slip st in next 2 sts*, (ch 3, picot, tr) in next st, tr in next st, (tr, picot, tr) in next st, tr in next st, (tr, picot, ch 3, slip st) in next st, slip st in next 2 sts, (ch 2, picot, dc) in next st; repeat from * to * once, (slip st, ch 6, sc in 2nd ch from hook and in next 4 ch, slip st) in next st (stem made), slip st in last 2 sts; join with slip st in base of beginning ch. Fasten off.

FINISHING
Weave in ends.

pineapple scrubby dishcloth

The pineapple is the symbol of welcoming and friendship. So it's the perfect scrubby to keep you company and be a partner in cleaning up kitchen messes. The Scrubby Sparkle yarn gives a twinkle to your crochet stitches and is the ideal texture to help your dishes sparkle!

Yarn
RED HEART® Scrubby Sparkle™, 3 oz (85 g), 174 yd (159 m) balls
- 1 ball each Lemon 8215 (A) and Avocado 8690 (B)

Hook
Susan Bates Crochet Hook®: 5.5 mm (US I-9)

Other
Yarn needle

LEARN BY VIDEO
www.go-crafty.com

Ch (chain)
Dc (double crochet)
Dc2tog (double crochet 2 stitches together)
Sc (single crochet)
Slip stitch
Tr (treble crochet)
Hdc (half double crochet)

Designed by Carolyn Calderon

GAUGE
13 dc = 4" (10 cm) and 13 rows dc = 8" (20 cm). CHECK YOUR GAUGE. Use any size hook to obtain the gauge.

MEASUREMENTS
Dishcloth measures 5" (12.5 cm) wide x 9" (23 cm) long (including Leaves)

SPECIAL TECHNIQUE
Join half double crochet with slip knot: Place a slip knot on the hook, yarn over, insert hook in indicated stitch, draw up a loop, pull yarn through 2 loops and slip knot to complete stitch.

DISHCLOTH
With A, ch 12; turn.
Row 1 (right side): Dc in 4th ch from hook (first 3 chs count as dc here and throughout), dc in each ch across; turn—10 dc.
Row 2: Ch 3, dc in next dc, 2 dc in next dc, dc in each of next 4 dc, 2 dc in next dc, dc in each of last 2 dc; turn—12 dc.
Row 3: Ch 3, dc in next dc, 2 dc in next dc, dc in each of next 6 dc, 2 dc in next dc, dc in each of last 2 dc; turn—14 dc.
Row 4: Ch 3, dc in each of next 5 dc, 2 dc in next dc, dc in each of last 7 dc, turn—15 dc.
Row 5: Ch 3, dc in each dc across; turn—15 dc.
Row 6: Ch 3, dc in each of next 6 dc, dc2tog, dc in each of last 6 dc; turn—14 dc.
Row 7: Ch 3, dc in each of next 5 dc, dc2tog, dc in each of last 6 dc; turn—13 dc.
Row 8: Ch 3, dc in each of next 4 dc, dc3tog, dc in each of last 5 dc—11 dc.
Row 9: Ch 3, dc in each of next 2 dc, dc2tog, dc in each of next 2 sts, dc2tog, dc in each of last 2 dc; turn—9 dc.
Row 10: Ch 3, dc in each st across; turn—9 dc.

EDGE
Ch 1 (does not count as a st), sc in each dc across top edge; 3 sc in corner; turn to work down first side, 2 sc around end of each row (dc) to next corner; 4 sc in corner; turn to work along bottom edge, sc in each st across to next corner; 4 sc in corner; turn to work up other side, 2 sc around end of each row to last corner; 3 sc in corner; slip st in top of beginning sc—73 sc. Fasten off yarn and weave in ends.

LEAVES
Row 1: Referring to photo for placement, join B with slip knot; hdc in 3rd ch from corner, dc in next sc, tr in next sc, dc in next sc, hdc in next sc; turn—5 sts.
Row 2: Ch 6, slip st in same st, ch 8, slip st in next st, ch 10, slip st in next st, ch 8, slip st in next st, ch 6, slip st in last st—5 chained loops.
Fasten off yarn and weave in ends.

watermelon slice scrubby

Crocheted in rounds, this watermelon Scrubby won't take long to make, but it will save you time at the kitchen sink. The polyester fiber is easy on your hands but tough on pots and pans. Keep it fresh by machine washing and air drying.

Yarn
RED HEART® Scrubby Sparkle™, 3 oz (85 g), 174 yd (159 m) balls
- 1 ball each 8929 Strawberry (A), 8690 Avocado (B), and 8012 Licorice (C)

Note Only a small quantity of B and C are needed for this project.

Hook
Susan Bates® Crochet Hook: 5.5 mm (US I-9)

Other
Yarn needle
Stitch marker
Fabric sealant (optional)

LEARN BY VIDEO
www.go-crafty.com
Ch (chain)
Sc (single crochet)
Slip stitch

Designed by Nancy Anderson

GAUGE
Gauge is not critical for this project.

MEASUREMENT
Scrubby measures 6½" in diameter.

SPECIAL TECHNIQUE
Join with sc: Place a slip knot on hook, insert hook in indicated stitch, yarn over and pull up a loop, yarn over and draw through both loops on hook.

SCRUBBY
With A, ch 2.

Round 1 (right side): Work 6 sc in 2nd ch from hook; join with slip st in first sc—6 sc.
Round 2: Ch 1, 2 sc in each st around; join with slip st in first sc—12 sc.
Round 3: Ch 1, sc in first st, 2 sc in next st, *sc in next st, 2 sc in next st; repeat from * around; join with slip st in first sc—18 sc.
Round 4: Ch 1, sc in first 2 sts, 2 sc in next st, *sc in next 2 sts, 2 sc in next st; repeat from * around; join with slip st in first sc—24 sc.
Round 5: Ch 1, sc in first 3 sts, 2 sc in next st, *sc in next 3 sts, 2 sc in next st; repeat from * around; join with slip st in first sc—30 sc.
Round 6: Ch 1, sc in first 4 sts, 2 sc in next st, *sc in next 4 sts, 2 sc in next st; repeat from * around; join with slip st in first sc—36 sc.
Round 7: Ch 1, sc in first 5 sts, 2 sc in next st, *sc in next 5 sts, 2 sc in next st; repeat from * around; join with slip st in first sc—42 sc.
Round 8: Ch 1, sc in first 6 sts, 2 sc in next st, *sc in next 6 sts, 2 sc in next st; repeat from * around; join with slip st in first sc—48 sc.
Round 9: Ch 1, sc in first 7 sts, 2 sc in next st, *sc in next 7 sts, 2 sc in next st; repeat from * around; join with slip st in first sc—54 sc. Fasten off.
Round 10: With right side facing, join B with sc in any st, sc in next 3 sts, *2 sc in next st, sc in next 8 sts; repeat from * around to last 4 sts, sc in last 4 sts; join with slip st in first sc—60 sc.
Round 11: Ch 1, sc in first 5 sts, *2 sc in next st, sc in next 9 sts; repeat from * around to last 4 sts, sc in last 4 sts; join with slip st in first sc—66 sc. Fasten off.

FINISHING
With C, embroider 2 straight stitches over any sc in Round 6, taking care to completely cover sc. On wrong side of piece, weave yarn through next 5 sts of same round and embroider 2 straight stitches over next sc. Repeat 4 times. Fasten off.

Weave in ends.
Optional: Apply a few drops of fabric sealant to ends of tails of seeds to prevent unraveling. ■

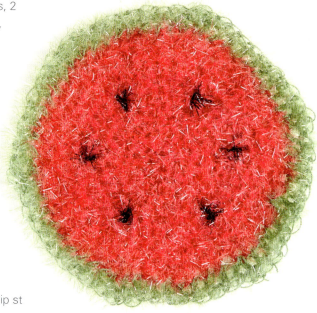